ENGLISH CHURCHES EXPLAINED

TREVOR YORKE

COUNTRYSIDE BOOKS
NEWBURY BERKSHIRE

First published 2010
© Trevor Yorke 2010
Reprinted 2016

All rights reserved. No reproduction
permitted without the prior permission
of the publisher:

COUNTRYSIDE BOOKS
3 Catherine Road
Newbury, Berkshire

To view our complete range of books,
please visit us at
www.countrysidebooks.co.uk

ISBN 978 1 84674 191 3

Photographs and illustrations by the author

Designed by Peter Davies, Nautilus Design
Produced through The Letterworks Ltd., Reading
Typeset by KT Designs, St Helens
Printed by The Holywell Press, Oxford

CONTENTS

Introduction

Some buildings are old. My last house was built in 1857 and its Victorian features and generations of occupants were part of its appeal. Some buildings are very old. Churches are very, very old, however, and the depth of history buried within their walls is breathtaking.

There are well over 10,000 which can trace their origins to the medieval period and many even further back in time. Take Brixworth church, for example: its first phase of construction took place barely a few hundred years after the Romans left; bricks from their buildings were used in its walls. It would have been a venerable edifice when William the Conqueror landed on these shores and over 900 years old when Henry VIII established the Church of England! Its stones have borne witness to Viking invaders, chivalrous knights, and battling Roundheads and Cavaliers. Yet, in the building you see today, there are traces of the incredible journey through time that this structure has taken. In its form and decoration can be unravelled the changes made to it by countless ambitious and powerful men over its 1,400 year life.

It was while drawing this building I first became aware of this vastness of time and that each arch and section of wall could be pinned to a stage in its development. I had always been fascinated by churches, but as a tool in landscape painting. So it came as a pleasant revelation when, after years of studying their form for artistic composition, I could begin to recognize them for their architectural value and date their various parts. This layman's book is an attempt to put the period styles of the church fabric and decoration into a simple-to-read form packed with photographs, pictures and diagrams.

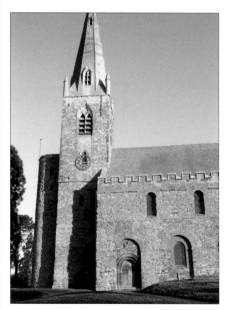

FIG 0.1 BRIXWORTH, NORTHANTS:
As is typical of most churches there is work from many ages, in this case from 7th-century arches to a 13th-century spire.

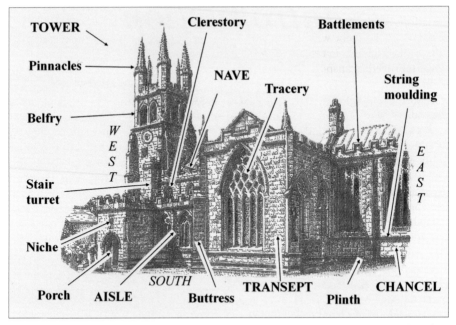

FIG 0.2: *Labels highlighting some of the features of a parish church mentioned in the book. Note the points of a compass as most old churches will be aligned on an east-west axis with the chancel containing the altar at the east end.*

The first section takes a journey through history, showing the changing architectural fashions and what you can see today. In each chapter is an imaginary church called 'Exemplar' which shows you what parish churches would have looked like in the relative periods. The second goes inside and explains the various fixtures and fittings within. There is also a final section with further information, a time chart and glossary of terms. The book focuses upon the secular side of the church and is intended to help the reader recognize the ordinary so they can better appreciate the extraordinary. The spiritual side is of such depth that this is left to other ecclesiastical publications, some of which are listed in the bibliography, while many others are available through Christian bookshops.

One element of a church which cannot be simplified into these neat compartments is the material it is made from. Those of medieval origin are vernacular buildings, erected with local materials and by local masons. The stone required for the walls had to be obtained from close at hand, only those with an extremely wealthy benefactor could afford to import it from outside the region. Those who built it probably were based in the area and rarely travelled far, so developed indigenous variations on the fashionable themes of the day. It was only with the appearance of the architect in the 18th century and improved transportation in the 19th that these vernacular forms were swept away by non regional styles and mass produced fittings.

Old churches stand today therefore as a record of the geological nature of the country. In the west there are notable outcrops of red sandstone, millstone grit along the Pennines and granite in the South-west. In a line from Dorset to Yorkshire runs a spine of limestone including the rich colours of the Cotswolds and Northamptonshire. To the east of this, good building stone is scarce and churches can be found with rough walls of flint, cobbles and chalk. This oversimplified plan is then peppered with localized outcrops, so even in an area of poor material you can suddenly come across a fine stone church. This variety is one of the great appeals of English churches, no one is the same as another. Yet, underlying this bewildering assortment, there are styles of feature and decoration which can be pinned down to a certain period. Turn over the next page and begin the journey through time and see what you can recognize the next time you pass by or visit a church.

Trevor Yorke

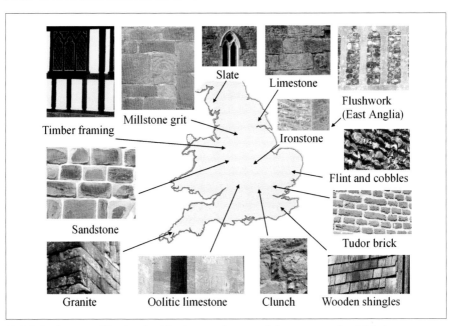

FIG 0.3: *A map of England with photos of some of the stonework which is distinctive of certain areas.*

Section I

Churches
through
the Ages

CHAPTER 1

Saxon and Norman Churches

—————— *AD 600–1200* ——————

FIG 1.1 BRASSINGTON, DERBYS: *This church set on the edge of the Peak District was built in the 12th century, yet as with most examples from this period the evidence is buried under later changes. The stocky, plain tower with its distinctive round-arch bell openings is the only part in this picture which is instantly recognizable as Norman.*

In the closing decades of the 6th century Britain found itself under invasion on two fronts. Not from further bands of pagan Saxons who over the previous hundred years had pushed the existing Romano-British and their culture into the West, but from Christian missionaries seeking to convert the population (in effect, to reintroduce a religion which had established itself in the last century of Roman rule). St Columba, who had travelled over from Ireland and founded a monastery on Iona in AD 563, and his followers influenced the North while Augustine, sent by the Pope, had landed in Kent in AD 597 and established a base in Canterbury (London was resolutely pagan!). The inevitable differences between the two as they spread across the country was ironed out at the Synod of Whitby in AD 664 and, over the following century, a system of a regional central minster dispatching preachers to outlying field churches or open air sites was created.

Viking raids and later invasion during the 9th century ruined monastic life and crippled the Church until Alfred and his successors forced them back and established England as a single state by the mid 10th century. Under Edgar (AD 944–975) church building flourished, now not just minsters but new, smaller estate buildings, as lesser nobles sought to gain higher status by erecting a church next to their manor house, a fashion which continued over the next 200 years. At the same time the payment of tithes to support the priests was put in law and a parish from which they were to be paid was established, many following the boundary of these local estates. The majority of our medieval parish churches are likely to have been founded this way by Saxon nobles and after the Conquest by Norman barons until the late 12th century when the old minster system was virtually obsolete.

Saxon Churches

Part of the success of the early missionaries is likely to have been due to their adoption of existing pagan religious sites, and many early churches were built alongside holy wells, ancient stones, burial mounds and Roman remains. They were usually simple rectangular structures, mostly built from timber and have long since gone (an exception is in Fig 1.17); those which survive are the ones built in

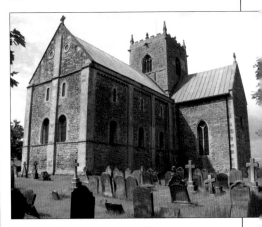

FIG 1.2 STOW, LINCS: *This outstanding example of a large Late Saxon cruciform church dwarfs the tiny village around it. Its size and dominant position are clues that it was once an important minster. These early principal churches were mainly established in the 7th and 8th centuries near important centres of the day and acted as a missionary base from which priests or monks could go out and preach to other communities within a territory. The creation of parishes from the 10th century broke down this system. Their presence is also still recorded in place-names like Kidderminster, or where they became a cathedral as at York Minster.*

stone. These relied upon the bulk of their walls for stability and the thickness was exposed at the windows which were typically small with many splayed on both sides so the shutter or material used to close them off was in the centre (glass was rare).

The main body had a distinctive tall, narrow form, most with a smaller chancel built onto the east end and a few larger churches having transepts to the sides and a tower. Where the wall had to be supported above a window, doorway or the opening between the nave and chancel, a simple round arch was used, typically narrow with tall sides. The roof above would have been steeply pitched and most likely thatched.

Most of what you see today from this period will be fragmentary. Of the couple of hundred churches that display their Saxon origin, this is usually only indicated by the distinctive narrow profile of a nave or a single round headed window.

FIG 1.3: *Churches built near ruined Roman towns or villas often raided their masonry (see Fig 1.18) for thin red bricks, then incorporated them into walls and arches as in this example at Brixworth (top). A distinctive feature of Late Saxon and Early Norman churches was the laying of stone in a herringbone pattern as in this example from Marton, Lincs (bottom).*

FIG 1.4: *A distinctive feature of Saxon churches was long and short work, where narrow stones were alternately placed vertically and then horizontally on the corners (quoins).*

FIG 1.6: *Doorways (and the chancel arch inside) were typically simple and narrow with a lack of confidence in the size of the round arch limiting their width. They have a large impost stone from where the arch springs and occasionally attached columns.*

FIG 1.5: *Windows were usually small with a single and occasionally a twin opening (often with an elongated barrel shaped baluster in the centre). Most had a round head, smaller ones crudely carved out of a single block (top), larger examples with the arch formed out of carved segments (centre). A unique form on some Saxon churches was the triangular head (bottom).*

FIG 1.7: *Columns and the capitals on top of them are only found in a few Saxon churches. They are simple in form, often with decorative carving (the Saxons were in some ways more skilled craftsmen than the later Normans).*

Norman Churches

William the Conqueror's bloody arrival on these shores was followed by a large-scale building of castles and cathedrals; imposing structures designed to leave the rebellious Saxon population in awe. Apart from these there were few major churches built, it was the continuing pattern of local lords erecting new places of worship alongside their manorial homes which dominates this period. Parish churches found next to earthworks of motte and bailey castles are a common remnant of this link. However, a drive for a more pious Church during the 12th century encouraged these secular owners of churches to surrender the rights they had to appoint priests and collect revenue for services (part of the motivation for many to build the church in the first place) and place them into the hands of bishops and monasteries.

These early Norman churches have much in common at first glance with the simple, narrow Saxon structures except

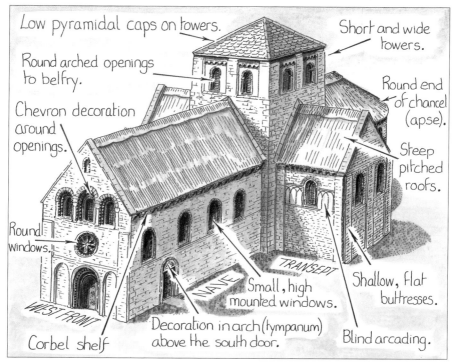

FIG 1.8: *Example of a large Norman church with labels of characteristic features. The exterior is shown covered in whitewash with colour painted around openings. Although this is just conjectural it is likely that many churches had some form of exterior coating and decoration.*

that an apse, a semi-circular extension to the chancel, was a popular import at this time from France. Towers were not common in most areas although on major buildings a cruciform plan with a central square structure above the crossing was a popular and distinctive feature. The round arch was always used for openings; the inability to make it wider without making it higher in proportion limited the width of windows and doors although there are a few impressive attempts at large chancel arches, albeit distorted! Where a wall had to be supported over a long space (usually between the nave and side aisles) a row of round arches was supported upon thick square piers or broad round columns, the latter with crude blocks at the base and plain capitals on top.

By the mid 12th century these churches suddenly begin to flourish with decoration and a distinctive Norman style emerges with vibrant geometric carvings.

FIG 1.10: *Important entrances had recessed doorways with receding arches, as in this example from Steetley, Derbys. The row of beakheads above are Norman in style but date to restoration around 1880.*

FIG 1.11: *Windows were either singles or in pairs under a round arch and set high up in the wall. The shutter or cloth (glass was too expensive for most parish churches at this date) was now on the outer edge so they had just a deep single splay on the inside. This example is a former belfry opening at Burford, Oxon, which has later been glazed.*

FIG 1.9: *Some doorways had a square head with the semi-circular space above (tympanum) filled with a carved pattern or scene as in this exceptional example from Kilpeck, Hereford.*

FIG 1.12: *The round arch was also used to decorative effect by forming a horizontal band of repeated or interlocking blank arches called blind arcading. They have been used here between the distinctive Norman belfry openings on a round tower. These feature mainly in Norfolk and Suffolk and are usually Saxon or Norman in date.*

FIG 1.13: *Corbels (stone brackets) were often fitted under the lower edge of a roof. These formed corbel tables or shelves (top) and are a distinctive feature of Norman churches. They were usually carved with heads and figures (bottom) as with these examples from Kilpeck, Hereford.*

FIG 1.14: *Later Norman churches were distinguished by decorative carving, most notably the zig zag or chevron pattern around arches. These usually point the eye towards the opening but can occasionally be found placed on their side around the arch, pointing outwards (see inner arch in Fig 1.11), a detail usually dating to around 1160. The example above shows bands from right (inner edge) to left of beakheads, chevrons, pellets (round beads) and billets (alternately spaced square blocks). Other decorative forms included diamond patterns, a band of rope design and lozenges (flat diamonds).*

FIG 1.15: *Norman columns were generally stocky but became gradually thinner compared with earlier types. They could be round or octagonal and sometimes alternate in the same arcade, some with patterns carved down them. Capitals usually had a square top, often with just a plain chamfered block below shaped like a cushion. This could be further decorated with scallops (left) or volutes (right) as in these late 12th-century examples from Youlgreave, Derbys.*

FIG 1.16 EXEMPLAR CHURCH c1100: *This first visit to Exemplar church shows the simple stone building with a thatched roof adjacent to the manor house (right), the residence of a Norman baron who was responsible for initiating its construction. It replaced a smaller timber structure which had been the first church on the site and had a rounded apse added onto the end of the chancel. The only feature in the churchyard is a stone cross, as graves rarely had permanent markers at this date.*

STILL OUT THERE

FIG 1.17 GREENSTED, ESSEX: *A unique survivor of a wooden church of which only the shortened vertical timbers in this picture date from the Saxon period. Most churches built in this period would have been in this material and it is only when later ones are excavated that the impression of the post holes of these earlier structures are sometimes found underneath.*

FIG 1.18 ESCOMB, COUNTY DURHAM: *One of only a few examples of largely unaltered Saxon churches with its distinctive tall, narrow nave and tiny windows (the large one in the centre and the narrow ones to the right are later additions). Roman masonry from nearby Binchester Fort is thought to have been used in Escomb's construction (note near the top of the wall it looks like they ran out and had to use smaller stones for the final courses).*

FIG 1.19 BRIXWORTH, NORTHANTS: *This largest surviving early Saxon church (late 7th-century) like many others suffered destruction by Vikings, typically during the late 8th and early 9th centuries. The apse in the foreground was rebuilt around AD 1000 with a polygonal shape (they could also be round or square). The main body has the distinctive tall, narrow shape although the top of the tower, the spire and pointed windows are later additions.*

FIG 1.20 EARLS BARTON, NORTHANTS: *One of a number of distinctive late Saxon towers with triangular and round headed openings, long and short work and decorative stone strips. These vertical pieces may be replicating a form of construction used on timber churches at the time. Towers were not common on parish churches in most areas except in East Anglia where distinctive round ones may have also played a defensive role (see Fig 1.12).*

FIG 1.21 STEWKLEY, BUCKS: *Later Norman churches are distinguished by a riot of carving and bold geometric decoration as in this west end of a largely unaltered church. The nave, tower and chancel in a single line with no transepts is a form associated with this period. Simple round windows as in the gable in this picture can often be found on larger Norman churches.*

FIG 1.22 KILPECK, HEREFORD: *This notable little church is famous for its carving but has also retained its original form, one which was typical of many smaller parish churches in the Norman period. Having the nave, chancel and apse in a line with just a belfry and no tower was repeated all across the country.*

FIG 1.23 STOW, LINCS: *A view from the nave looking towards the chancel at the far end of the interior of this Saxon minster church most likely dating from just before the Norman Conquest. The round arch in the foreground has the distinctive tall and narrow profile and the windows to the side are deeply splayed and high up in the walls. The space just beyond the arch is the crossing, the area under the tower, which in large Saxon churches was the climax of the building (the pointed arch you can see dates from a later period, probably when the tower was heightened).*

FIG 1.24 TICKENCOTE, RUTLAND: *This tiny church is a feast of Norman decoration yet most dates from an exuberant 18th-century restoration. The major part they left untouched was this huge chancel arch which despite sagging in the middle has stood for more than 800 years. It is distinctive Late Norman work with receding arches decorated with chevrons, beakheads and billets and narrow cushion capitals carved with scallops and symbols.*

FIG 1.25 BAKEWELL, DERBYS: *A view of the west end of the nave arcade showing on the right a narrow, round Norman arch with thick square piers and prominent impost stone and on the left a later pointed arch with much thinner columns (actually Victorian but based on medieval work). It illustrates what you will find in the next chapter, that the pointed arch helped make the interior of churches lighter and more spacious.*

CHAPTER 2

Early English and Decorated Churches

1200–1350

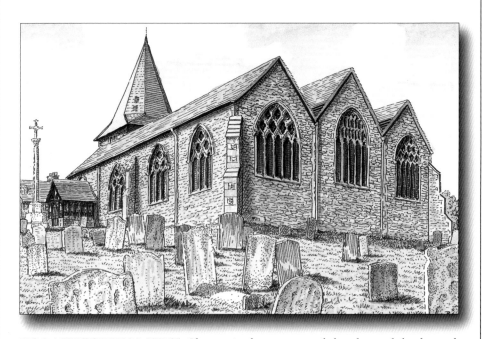

FIG 2.1 WESTERHAM, KENT: *Changes in the structure of churches and the demand from a growing congregation during this period suddenly transformed many church interiors from narrow and gloomy to spacious and colourful. This example displays some of the new features from this period like larger windows with tracery and prominent buttresses along the walls. It also has the distinctive triple roofs over the nave and aisles, which was common on Kent and Cornish churches, and the splay foot spire made of wood and originally covered with oak shingles, which was popular in the South-East during this period.*

The 13th century was the golden age of the medieval period. The population grew, harvests were good, markets were established in towns, and there was money to be made from exporting wool, especially in the Eastern counties whose ports were close to the Low Countries where there was demand from its weavers. This wealth was reflected in the churches of areas like Northamptonshire and Lincolnshire, although the pressure for more room for a growing congregation meant that all over the country naves and chancels were rebuilt and side aisles added.

The Church itself had changed from that when William the Conqueror landed in 1066, as under the influence of successive Popes it had separated itself from the direct influence of kings and encouraged a return to the true faith. The result on the ground was that the nobility who had built vast numbers of parish churches, some with half an eye on the profit which could be made from services, found income drying up as the influence of these reforms directed payment away from their coffers and so they began handing control of them over to bishops and abbots. By the beginning of this period only a small number of churches were still in private hands (known as peculiars), while those now under the jurisdiction of monasteries benefited from their wealth and a more up-to-date style of architecture. The key ingredient of the new form of building in this period was the pointed arch.

FIG 2.2 EMPINGHAM, LEICS: *This imposing village church in the East Midlands, which blossomed in this period from the trade in wool, probably gained its grand dimensions from being next to one of the Bishop of Lincoln's palaces. Many of the most impressive churches in this period may have benefited from association with bishops and abbots.*

Early English

In cathedrals and abbeys from the mid-12th century the round arch can be found alongside the new pointed arch in a transitional period which ended with the general adoption of the latter in the first half of the 13th century (Canterbury Cathedral was the most influential). The pointed arch gave the mason greater flexibility as the width or height could be altered independently of each other, unlike the round arch where they could only be adapted in unison (to make the opening wider you had to make it higher).

Another problem was countering the action of the heavy sloping roof which will naturally try and push the walls below outwards. The Normans simply built the walls very thick, relying upon

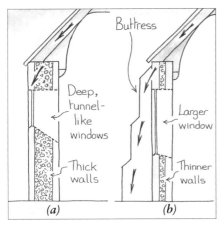

FIG 2.3: *Diagram showing a section through a Norman wall (left) and one from the 14th century (right). The arrows mark the outward thrust from the roof which is countered by the sheer mass of the wall in the first example but by buttresses in the later one, allowing walls to be thinner and windows larger.*

their bulk and the steep pitch of the roof to counter the action (Fig 2.3a). With the introduction of the pointed arch which directs most of the load vertically, and with the use of buttresses along the outside wall (Fig 2.3b), the outward thrust was better controlled. As a result walls could become thinner and openings in them larger. This created a lighter space inside with thinner columns and more graceful detailing, making the body of the building less gloomy and more elegant.

The earliest phase of what is generally termed Gothic architecture (a derisory term used by later exponents of Classical architecture for buildings

featuring the pointed arch) is known as Early English and this new style spanned most of the 13th century. Its notable feature is the lancet window; tall, thin openings with a pointed arch, usually set as singles or doubles down the side and then grouped in threes or fives on an end wall. By the mid century pairs were positioned together under a single arched moulding and the space

FIG 2.4 KETTON, RUTLAND: *This notable example of Early English architecture with its distinctive lancet windows is crowned by a huge broach spire. The broaches are the small triangular sections at the base which cover the gaps in the corners between the octagonal spire and the square tower upon which it sits. It is distinctive of the East Midlands where suitable stone and wealth combined in this period although the Victorians were so impressed with this particular example that they used it as a model for churches nationwide.*

FIG 2.5: *Doorways in the 13th century now had acute pointed arches with mouldings which were deep cut and filled with dog tooth decoration. Shafts up the sides could have plain or stiff leaf capitals and this example has been further embellished with blank lancets.*

between them was punctured with an opening to create plate tracery (see Fig 2.6).

It was common in this period to expand the building by adding an aisle along the side of the nave, usually on the north side first and later the south. The chancel was often enlarged, replacing the earlier semi-circular apse with a square end and a new larger east window. Towers were still not widespread and usually feature on major churches or those in wealthy areas like the East Midlands, where the distinctive broach spire which slightly overlaps the structure below, developed in this period (see Chapter 8). Doorways were now made with steep pitched pointed arches; the moulding around the edge was deep and often featured shafts up the jambs (sides) with a hollowed pyramid pattern known as dog tooth decorating the edges.

FIG 2.6: *Lancet windows, either as a single opening (left) or a group of three (centre), five and occasionally seven, are distinctive of the first half of the 13th century. In the second half, they were gathered under a single hood mould and the blank gap above the lancets was pierced by a round opening to create plate tracery (right), in this case with a quatrefoil, a four-lobed clover-leaf shape (the lobes are known as foils).*

FIG 2.7: *The hollowed out pyramid shape inserted between the mouldings is known as dog tooth and is a distinctive feature of Early English churches.*

FIG 2.8: *Columns were thinner than in the previous century and could be round (left), occasionally octagonal, or have a cluster of shafts carved around them (right) in larger churches (made from dark Purbeck marble in the finest). Some of these shafts had a profile like the hull of a ship and are referred to as keel moulded. Arcades were formed with acute pointed arches often with a double chamfer (left).*

FIG 2.9: *Capitals could be plain and round (top) with deep mouldings especially underneath (there was no square block above as there was on Norman examples). A rigid plant pattern known as stiff leaf (centre) was also popular. Bases had a distinctive groove on the top known as water holding moulding (bottom).*

Decorated

From the late 13th century the Gothic began to lose its rather austere appearance and became more ornate, with this next stage thus known as the Decorated period. Churches built from the 1280s up to around 1350 tend to have an emphasis on width rather than height; aisles which were added or re-built are broader than before and openings in the wall wider. Spires were a popular feature for those parishes with a wealthy benefactor, broach types still being used in some parts, but in the 14th century a new kind of spire recessed behind a parapet was more widespread. Small incised globes known as ballflowers were a distinctive decorative detail which can be found around openings, especially doorways, and usually date from the first half of the 14th century. Towards the end of this period the ogee arch was introduced, where the lower half curves inwards and then the upper part curves out to meet at a point, and can be found on doorways and belfry openings.

It is the windows of this period, however, which are the most distinctive and outstanding feature. In the matter of a few generations simple lancets had

Parapet spires popular on Decorated churches.

Simplified version of window tracery on belfry openings.

Groups of lancets and blind arcading used on Early English west fronts.

Aisles added to sides of nave (wider versions in 14th century).

Longer, square ended chancel

Towers mostly plain and short in 13th century

CHANCEL

Elaborate intersecting tracery on Decorated churches.

TRANSEPT

NAVE

AISLE

Stepped buttresses

Plate tracery in 13th century

Early English doorways have steep pitched pointed arches with shafts, deep moulding and dogtooth decoration.

FIG 2.10: *A large parish church as it may have appeared in this period with some of its characteristic features highlighted.*

FIG 2.11: *Hollowed globular decorations known as ballflowers are characteristic of Decorated churches, especially in the early 14th century.*

developed into masses of elaborate intersecting patterns. The first step was putting a single arched hood mould (these were designed to keep rainwater off the opening below) over a group of lancets rather than each individual one, which left a gap above which could neatly be filled in by cutting through a small window. This plate tracery was replaced in turn by similar patterns but formed from carved ribs of stone (bar or geometrical tracery). By the turn of the early 14th century the greater freedom these gave the masons meant they could create elaborate patterns, usually either a repeated arched pattern known as intersecting tracery or a series of linked 'S' shapes forming a net called reticulated tracery (actually formed out of intersecting ogee arches). By the mid 1300s a non-regular pattern which appears like mis-shaped tear drops and is known as curvilinear or flowing tracery was the finest display of the mason's art.

FIG 2.12: *Examples of Decorated windows with tracery from the geometric (left) – in which bars replaced the solid parts of plate tracery – which quickly developed into new forms like intersecting (centre) and reticulated (right). Earlier examples had plain circles in the head of the arch but from the late 13th century they are more likely to have cusps; these are small curved pieces along the sides of the bars which form leaf-like patterns in the openings (see the right-hand example). Each lobe formed is referred to as a foil, hence three lobes are called a trefoil.*

FIG 2.14: *An elaborate doorway at Boston, Lincs which shows the Decorated style at its flamboyant best. The ogee arch which curves in and then out to meet at a point is characteristic of this period (and was still popular in the next). The niches up the sides are now empty but originally would have held painted and gilded statues of saints and notable churchmen but these were usually destroyed after the Reformation (see Chapter 4).*

FIG 2.13: *Flowing or curvilinear tracery was the high point of the Decorated style and dates from the mid-14th century with incredibly complicated serpentine patterns enhanced by cusps.*

FIG 2.15: *A 14th-century parapet spire, so named as the junction between it and the square tower was hidden behind battlements (this made maintenance easier as ladders could rest upon the top of the tower). In order to remove water that fell behind the parapet, openings were made to drain it off and these had hollowed statues known as gargoyles to keep the water away from the foundations below. Hook-shaped protrusions up the angles of the spire, called crockets, were also popular in this period.*

FIG 2.16: *Piers were octagonal or square with four or eight attached half shafts (four are shown above). Pointed arches above had shallower mouldings than before. Flat strips down the centre of shafts, called fillets, were used in the late 13th and early 14th centuries.*

FIG 2.17: *Capitals could either be plain with moulded rings or have a more realistic foliage pattern which can be recognized as a specific tree like oak and maple. Human figures can also be found. Note the fillet running down the shaft in the foreground.*

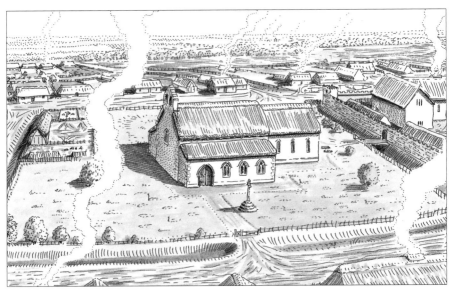

FIG 2.18 EXEMPLAR CHURCH c1300: *The village has expanded so the church has new aisles added to each side to increase capacity and a new longer chancel with narrow lancet windows. The priest now has his own house within the churchyard (top left) with pens for his livestock.*

STILL OUT THERE

FIG 2.19 WEST WALTON, NORFOLK: *A spectacular detached Early English tower with narrow lancets, plate tracery, belfry opening (see Fig 2.6) and acute pointed arch doorway. The tower was built separate from the church as the foundations were poor.*

FIG 2.20 STAMFORD, LINCS: *An elaborate tower stacked with lancet blind arcading and crowned by a broach spire.*

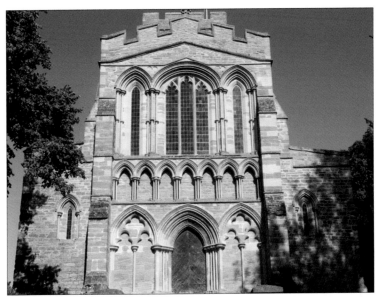

FIG 2.21 FELMERSHAM, BEDS: *An excellent example of an Early English parish church, with a notable west front in this view. Lancets, blind arcading and plate tracery embellish this ceremonial entrance to the building. Note that the aisles to each side are quite narrow.*

FIG 2.22 KEGWORTH, LEICS: *A little-altered Decorated church with parapet spire, wide aisles and windows with distinctive reticulated (centre) and intersecting tracery (right). The openings in the spire are known as spire lights and are important to ventilate the interior to avoid damp rot in the wooden structure below.*

FIG 2.23 NANTWICH, CHESHIRE:
A large town church which dates mainly from the 14th century. The windows in the foreground have distinctive flowing tracery and ogee arch moulding above. Octagonal towers were popular in this period with large Decorated belfry openings and ogee arch moulding above.

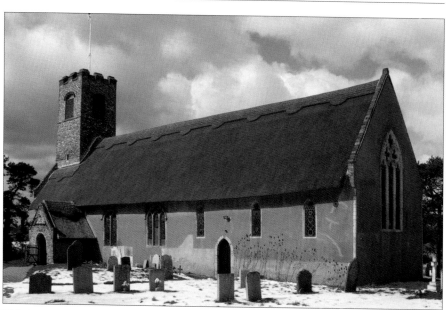

FIG 2.24 THURTON, NORFOLK: *A good example of a church which appears today as many would have originally: thatched roof, rendered walls, and windows dating from the early 14th century.*

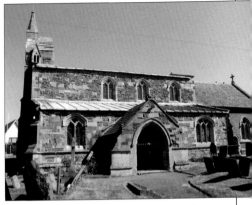

FIG 2.26 BURTON LAZARS, LEICS:
Many churches in this period would still have been modest in size and would not have had a tower. This example does, though, have a bellcote, while others had a timber bell cage freestanding in the churchyard. Twin bellcotes are a distinctive feature of East Leicestershire and Rutland churches.

FIG 2.25 HECKINGTON, LINCS:
A wonderful Decorated porch doorway with a band of flowing foliage wrapped around heraldic symbols and figures above the distinctive pointed arch.

FIG 2.27 HEXHAM, NORTHUMBERLAND: *The interior of this imposing church with characteristic Early English narrow openings. The middle row of openings, known as a triforium, was common on large Norman churches but rare thereafter. Note the deep moulding in the arches and the square section on the top of the capitals (abacus).*

CHAPTER 3

Perpendicular Churches
1350-1530

FIG 3.1 HIGH BRADFIELD, SOUTH YORKS: *Pinnacles, parapets, buttresses and prominent towers distinguish the last phase of Gothic architecture, the Perpendicular. This church also exhibits the flatter roofs which are characteristic of this period, permitting a row of extra windows, the clerestory, to be inserted above the side aisles and making the interior lighter and more spacious.*

If the 13th century was a high point for the population of England, then the 14th century was certainly its lowest. Terrible harvests after 1315, then the Black Death from 1348 and its regular recurrence over the following decades reduced numbers by up to a half in some places. Nor were these calamities selective, with aristocrats and the clergy just as likely to be affected as the peasants. The resulting lack of manpower for agriculture began the slow process of breaking down the feudal system, permitting those from a less fortunate background to escape from their home village servitude, some within a few generations creating themselves a family fortune. With monasteries and aristocrats often crippled by loss of numbers and falling incomes from rent and gifts, it was the new gentry class, notably wool merchants, that often financed new church building.

The fear of mortality and a preoccupation with the afterlife was expressed in the churches of the period. The rich had always bestowed gifts upon the clergy to ease their passage through purgatory, but now they established chantry chapels in their parish churches where mass could be celebrated for the soul of its founder (it was chanted, hence chantry chapel). Memorials of the wealthy often had an open section below the life-size effigy in which was placed a carved skeleton (cadaver), a humble reminder that they

FIG 3.2 WINSCOMBE, SOMERSET: *Wool was still big business, except now rather than being exported as a raw material it was woven in England, with areas like the Cotswolds, Somerset and Suffolk benefiting most from the trade. Merchants working here and in the ports where the cloth was exported financed the building of new naves (the chancel was still regarded as the property of the clergy), chapels and most notably huge west towers, as in this lavish example.*

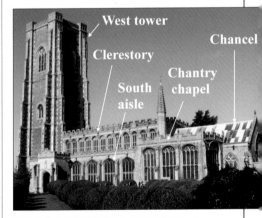

FIG 3.3 LAVENHAM, SUFFOLK: *A distinctive feature of this period was the provision of a chantry chapel. In some, a section of the existing building was set aside or rebuilt to accommodate the altar where mass would be celebrated for the founder's soul. In others, a new separate structure was added, usually onto one side of the chancel, as here.*

too will suffer the same fate as the poor. Doom paintings above the chancel arch were ghoulish reminders to the illiterate masses in the nave of what could befall those who strayed from the right path.

Despite this apparent gloom and despair the churches of this period are the most glorious and memorable ever built. The spectacular work of the mason was now matched by that of the carpenter and glazier as the interior of the church became as important as its exterior. Wide and ornate screens between the nave and chancel and elaborate displays of colourful stained glass illuminated a space designed to be lighter and more spacious. Chancel arches and openings into the aisles were larger with narrow columns devoid of capitals directing the eye to a row of windows along the top of the nave, called a clerestory. This was only possible in many churches because of the development of guttering and the use of lead sheets, which meant the roof above could be flatter so the nave walls could be extended above the line of the aisle roof. This also meant that a parapet could run around the exterior with gargoyles added at regular intervals to throw any rainwater away from the walls below. Buttresses were even more important to support walls weakened by these larger openings and they became deeper, with numerous steps to help deflect rain away, but at the same time were thinner than earlier types.

A distinguishing feature of the Perpendicular church is the use of vertical bars (mullions) running the full height of the window. This began in the

FIG 3.4: *Parapets were a popular feature of Perpendicular churches, which tend to either have patterns carved out of a solid wall (left) or battlements (right). Pinnacles (left) and gargoyles (right) were also popular.*

mid-14th century, often still with some curved bars in the upper part reflecting a transition from the previous Decorated style and, by the 15th century, the vertical bars are divided into smaller rectangular panels. The pointed arch became gradually flatter through this period, beginning similar to that of the Decorated and ending with a wider emphasis, created with a tight radius at its lower end (springing) and then a large radius in the middle, known as a four-centred arch (see Fig 3.8). By the turn of the 16th century, windows with a square head and a hood mould above were common. The ogee arch (formed from two reversed 'S' shapes) remained popular for windows, belfry openings and doorways. Porches were often added or rebuilt in this period with flat roofs and elaborate decoration, some with a room above providing accommodation for a priest, a school or store room.

The most outstanding feature of this period, however, is the tower. Although many were built before, it was now that they became a dominant fashion accessory for competing local congregations. Existing squat towers were heightened with pinnacles, parapets and large stepped buttresses added or new ones built from scratch, with string courses dividing its soaring mass into stages. Belfry openings tended to be larger than before and there can be much decoration at the top although the bulk of the tower could be plain, fine cut masonry. It was also usual for these huge structures to be added to the west end and, as they were so tall, spires seemed unnecessary and are rare at this date.

FIG 3.5: *Although earlier ones can be found, it is from this period that most of our surviving medieval porches date. As they were often added to an existing aisle or nave, the inner doorway will be older while the outer opening could be lavishly decorated as in this example from Burford, Oxon.*

FIG 3.6: *West towers were a key feature of the age, divided by horizontal mouldings into stages with large belfry openings. Buttresses in the corners were important for support and were thinner but deeper than before, with numerous steps. Some were decorated with niches which originally would have held statues.*

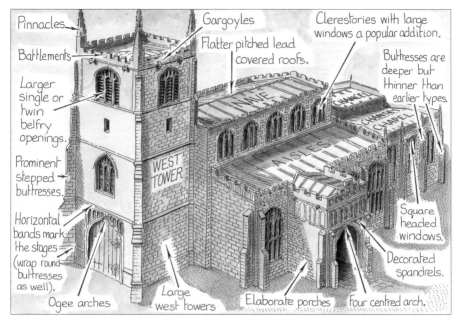

Pinnacles

Battlements

Larger single or twin belfry openings.

Prominent stepped buttresses.

Horizontal bands mark the stages (wrap round buttresses as well).

Ogee arches

WEST TOWER

Gargoyles

Flatter pitched lead covered roofs.

Clerestories with large windows a popular addition.

Buttresses are deeper but thinner than earlier types.

NAVE

CHANCEL

CHANTRY CHAPEL

AISLES

Square headed windows.

Decorated spandrels.

Large west towers

Elaborate porches

Four centred arch.

FIG 3.7: *A large Perpendicular church, with labels of characteristic features.*

FIG 3.8: *Late 14th-century windows still have steep arches and curved elements in the top but have a more pronounced vertical emphasis (left) to the tracery than in earlier Decorated types. In the following century they tended to be wider with vertical bars (mullions) running the full height and flatter four-centred arches above (centre). Later types sometimes have square heads (right), Horizontal bars (transoms) to strengthen the windows are also characteristic of the age.*

FIG 3.9: *Doorways usually had a pointed arch (left), a flatter four-centred one (above) or an ogee arch under a square hood or band of decoration. The triangular sections to the sides of the arch (spandrels) were filled with carved figures or heraldry, the latter a popular decorative feature. The mouldings in the arch tended to have wide shallow hollows, some with square flowers inserted between the ribs which run down the jambs, usually with no capitals.*

FIG 3.10: *Piers were slimmer at first, octagonal, often with half shafts attached and capitals above, which were usually moulded (left). Later examples often have the moulding up the piers continuing under the arch with either small or no capitals (right). Arcades have slightly flatter arches than before.*

FIG 3.11: *The square flower motif was a distinctive decorative detail from this period. It is usually found in the wide, shallow gaps in mouldings around doorways and with large gaps between.*

FIG 3.12: *Vaulted ceilings formed from stone ribs were an expensive luxury rarely found in parish churches (except those which were formerly monastic) but in this period can sometimes be found in chapels and porches. They could be a rib vault (left) with a decorative boss covering the central joint or a fan vault (right), the finest example of the mason's art.*

FIG 3.13 EXEMPLAR CHURCH c1500: *The Black Death has left the village reduced in size but many of those who survived have prospered and poured their money into the church. The nave and aisles have been rebuilt with a new flatter roof and a west tower added; however, the clergy have spent little upon the chancel which remains largely as before.*

STILL OUT THERE

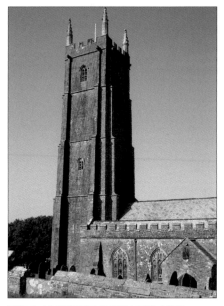

FIG 3.14 LONG MELFORD, SUFFOLK: *This famous parish church was largely built in the late 15th century with the flat-roofed nave, large clerestory windows and deeply buttressed aisle distinctive of the age. The triple-gabled addition in the foreground is a Lady Chapel added around 1500, while the tower was rebuilt at the turn of the 20th century. The south and east sides are faced in stone and knapped flint (cut to give a flat outer surface) which is formed into patterns known as flushwork.*

FIG 3.15 STOKE IN HARTLAND, DEVON: *Built in the early 15th century, this example has the distinctive Perpendicular features of prominent buttresses, string courses and battlements.*

FIG 3.16 CHIPPING CAMPDEN, GLOS: *The distinctive warm Cotswold limestone with pinnacles, battlements and large west tower are characteristic of wool churches built in this area. The original church was rebuilt in the late 15th century and was probably completely financed by wealthy merchants and clothiers in the then busy town.*

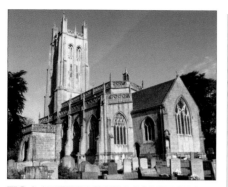

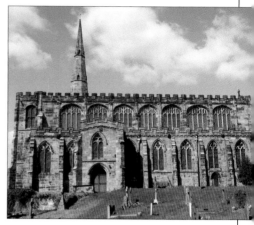

FIG 3.17 WRINGTON, SOMERSET: *Of all counties, none has such a spectacular display of towers as Somerset, so much so that they are usually subdivided into numerous local types. Financed mainly by the wool industry in this period, they are often elaborately decorated with large belfry openings, as in this example, with the nave and aisles receiving similar Perpendicular treatment. The small bellcote at the east end of the nave housed a Sanctus bell, which was rung at various times during mass.*

FIG 3.18 ASTBURY, CHESHIRE: *This imposing village church displays the change in style, with windows greatly enlarged. The lower set of windows on the aisle date from around 1300, with simple geometric tracery, but the clerestory windows above are much larger with hardly any wall between them and date from the rebuilding of the nave, probably in the late 15th century.*

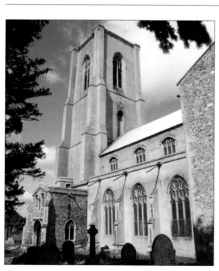

FIG 3.19 CAWSTON, NORFOLK: *A church in part rebuilt with money left by the Earl of Suffolk, the Lord of the Manor from 1385. Its distinctive Perpendicular tower (although strangely plain) and south porch bear his coat of arms, heraldic symbols being a particular feature of this period.*

FIG 3.20 TONG, SHROPSHIRE: *A collegiate church rebuilt in the 15th century by the widow of the Lord of the Manor, in which mass could be chanted for his soul. This was a popular foundation in this period, with a college for a small number of priests attached to a grand church. The buildings once to the right of this view have all gone now but almshouses, often included in the package, do survive in part.*

FIG 3.21 LAVENHAM, SUFFOLK: *The real wonder of Perpendicular architecture is the interior. Large clerestory and aisle windows allowed light to pour into the spacious nave with its distinctive timber beam ceiling and illuminated the work of the carpenter and glazier, as well as that of the mason. Originally the interior would have been colourfully-painted, including the ceilings, many of which would have been further embellished with carved bosses, decorative panels and wooden angels flying from where the beams meet the wall.*

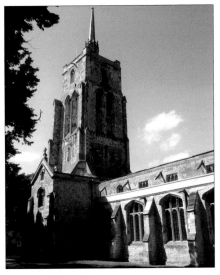

FIG 3.22 ASHWELL, HERTS: *A church with 15th-century features including the belfry openings, south aisle windows and two-storey porch, but one which is more famous for the graffiti carved inside the base of the tower. It records the horrific events as the Black Death ravaged the area and includes a unique view of old St Paul's cathedral.*

CHAPTER 4

Tudor, Stuart and Georgian Churches
——1530–1830——

FIG 4.1 LONGNOR, STAFFS: *Georgian churches, like this example dating from 1780, are distinctive by their nave and chancel being all in one huge body with no aisles and the use of Classical forms like columns and round arched windows. Despite the dominance of this style from antiquity, Gothic details as on the tower here at Longnor were used, and increasingly so towards the end of this period.*

Henry VIII's attempts to seek a divorce from his first wife and the subsequent separation from both her and the Catholic Church had a dramatic effect across England.

Although the King had played upon doubts and grievances which already existed towards the clergy, the changes which resulted from the establishment of the Church of England and the

Dissolution of the Monasteries during the 1530s must have shocked congregations cut off from the tumultuous Court circles. This Reformation changed the service from a mysterious ceremony performed in Latin and largely out of view behind the rood screen (a wooden or stone barrier between the nave and chancel with a large crucifix, the rood, upon it) to one where a sermon was preached by the priest from his pulpit in their native tongue. Over the next 100 years, during various zealous bouts of

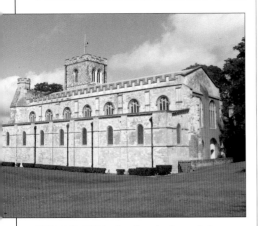

FIG 4.2: *With the dissolution of the monasteries the old abbey or priory church was often given to the parish. Many of our churches may have originally been monastic but as they might then have been found too large for local needs only a section was used, with the other parts demolished or falling into ruin. Here at Dunstable Priory the nave with its aisles was retained while the central tower (which stood at the right end where the red brick is) and the chancel beyond were knocked down.*

destruction by county commissioners and others, the interior of most churches was transformed from a richly coloured, dark and imposing experience to one which was bright and sanitized with whitewashed walls, an open plan, and clear glass in the windows.

The physical structure of most churches now entered a period of stagnation and decline as the driving forces behind medieval rebuilding, like the monasteries, had gone or turned their attention elsewhere. This was particularly true of the local gentry who with the banning of chantry chapels during the Reformation began to lose interest in financing their local church and displayed their steadily increasing wealth upon grand new country houses instead. In most cases later Tudor and Stuart building was limited to replacing parts of churches which had become unsafe or had fallen down. There were few complete churches put up until the devastation caused by the Great Fire of London forced the Commissioners to turn to Sir Christopher Wren to rebuild the 50 or so medieval structures engulfed by the flames.

There were sweeping changes in both village and town during the Georgian period. The setting of the country house became as important as its façade and the creation of great parks resulted in the sweeping away of whole villages, usually leaving the old parish church stranded or rebuilt on a new site. Their crumbling Gothic structures hardly fitted in with the owner's new Classical mansion so they either added a few of

FIG 4.4: *A key element in designing parks around country houses was the use of eye catchers or follies, structures which would surprise visitors or mark out the extensive boundary of the owner's land. Others just wanted to improve the view of their imaginary Roman world – they saw themselves as descendants of Roman nobles and not medieval knights. Like many country house owners Sir Francis Dashwood decided the old medieval church on top of the hill overlooking his new house at West Wycombe was inappropriate and transformed it by rebuilding the nave and tower but leaving the chancel, still the domain of the clergy. He also added a huge golden ball on top in which it is claimed his notorious Hellfire Club could convene.*

FIG 4.3: *Sir Christopher Wren (1632–1723) started life, as many early architects did, in another career, in his case as a talented scientist who suddenly after a few amateur designs found himself responsible for the rebuilding of London's churches in the wake of the Great Fire of 1666. His designs were ingenious and varied from the Baroque masterpiece of St Paul's Cathedral to his inventive steeples, as in this example from St Bride's (said to be the inspiration for the modern wedding cake). These were the first Classical places of worship built for the Church of England and set the standard for the next 150 years. At the peak of the rebuilding there were nearly 30 under construction all at the same time and most of the 51 he designed were complete by 1686.*

the latest fashionable trimmings like a cupola on the tower or built a new church, retaining little of the old.

A rapidly growing, urban population had put pressure upon the Church to respond, but apart from the physical

FIG 4.5: *Chapels were a distinctive feature of the 18th and 19th centuries. Some, as with this example in the Peak District, were built for remote communities, others were for the new dissenting groups like the Baptists and Methodists. Most were simple, symmetrical structures with a large body, galleries within and simple round arched windows.*

celibacy, now he could be a member of the upper classes, a married man who demanded a fine house for his family which was suitable for entertaining the circles in which they mixed. In many towns and villages the most notable church building from this period will be the vicarage!

Tudor, Stuart and Georgian Churches

What little was built in the 100 years after the Reformation was still similar in form to that which preceded it, except square-headed windows were widely used. The most obvious difference, however, was in the use of brick, at this stage usually confined to the south and east but by the 18th century the most common material, even if then it was faced over with stone or rendered to look like it.

With the restoration of the monarchy in 1660, the Classical style which had previously only been tentatively used became dominant and in the aftermath of the Great Fire of London it was mastered by Wren on his churches. The round arch returned with large prominent voussoirs (the segments from which arches are composed) while later ones might have just the central keystone highlighted. Windows were large rectangular grids of clear glass, usually with a semi-circular head, while external walls were composed of fine-cut masonry with some of the more lavish having pilasters (flat columns attached to the wall).

Another notable change was in the form of the nave and chancel. No longer were they required to be

rebuilding of naves and the fitting of galleries inside to increase capacity, they did little for these new congregations' hearts and minds. This inactivity aided the expansion of dissenting groups like the Methodists and Baptists and the erecting of thousands of chapels, especially in the late 18th and 19th centuries, is a key feature of the new townscapes.

The remoteness of many of the clergy towards the changing times was partly because by now it was seen as a position suitable for the sons of aristocrats and gentry. Gone was the poor medieval parish priest bound to

FIG 4.6: *Although brick had been used in a few eastern counties like Essex before the Reformation, it was in this period that its use became widespread. In Tudor times it was still regarded as a luxury product and was often cut to form door and window surrounds, as in this 16th-century example. Tudor bricks were handmade, usually on site from local clay; they tend to be thin, irregular and set in a thick line of mortar. By the Georgian period they had become standardized and set in regular bonds but as they became more common were often covered in render to imitate stone.*

separate as the service was now performed directly in front of the congregation, so new churches and chapels erected to meet the demands of a growing population or to replace dilapidated buildings had it all under one roof in a distinctive large rectangular structure. To increase capacity, aisles were not added as in the medieval church but an internal gallery was built down the sides and above the west end (strictly speaking, columns were still used to support the now massive single flat pitched roof and so form aisles up the sides, although not defined as such). Towers were still built on larger churches, some with exuberant stacking of columns and a spire or just a simple cupola on top. The structure below was generally plain with a wide belfry opening, round-arched in most but with a flat point and 'Y'-shaped tracery on late 18th- and early 19th-century Gothick types (the 'k' is added to differentiate this style from Victorian Gothic).

FIG 4.7: *From the late 17th century it became common for the architect who designed an aristocrat's main residence to have some influence over the church which often stood nearby, as here at Witley Court, Worcs. These were now at the mercy of the owner's whims and show the latest architectural styles from the flamboyant Baroque to the austere Neoclassical, with the architect replacing the mason as the designer of churches. The use of foreign styles and, towards the end of the period, materials from outside the local area also brought an end to vernacular building.*

FIG 4.8: *The Baroque was the dominant style in the late 17th and early 18th centuries, as pictured here at St Philip's Cathedral, Birmingham (consecrated as a parish church in 1715). Giant pilasters, tall windows, balustraded parapets with vases, and exuberant decoration are key features.*

FIG 4.9: *Palladian architecture was popular in the mid-18th century, as here at Gibside, County Durham, dating from the 1760s. It was a more refined style, concentrating on correct proportions rather than rich decoration.*

FIG 4.10: *In the late 18th and early 19th centuries the Neoclassical style influenced church building, as in this example from Buxton, Derbys. Classical forms were used in new ways and buildings can appear austere with decoration often limited to towers and large porticos across the end of the building (the one in the right of this picture was later filled in).*

FIG 4.11: *Despite the domination of Classical styles, Gothic forms were used, at first inaccurate replications of details applied to a Classical building as in this example from Stone, Staffs, with the distinctive 'Y'-shaped window tracery. By the early 19th century it became more than just a decoration.*

FIG 4.12 EXEMPLAR CHURCH c1800: *Although the village has grown, once again the church remains much as before and signs of neglect are visible. A new round-arched porch and a cupola on top of the tower are the only additions, although a fine new vicarage has been built behind the churchyard and a manor house to the right.*

STILL OUT THERE

FIG 4.13 MACCLESFIELD, CHESHIRE: *Most Georgian churches were built as part of a country estate or to service expanding new towns as here at Christchurch, Macclesfield, opened in 1776. In this period, buildings like this were usually paid for by local gentry or industrialists: it was Charles Roe, who is regarded as the founder of the town's silk industry, who financed this structure which looms over the neighbouring terraces. It is a standard Classical form but with an exceptionally tall tower featuring a Gothic-style ogee arch belfry opening.*

FIG 4.14 ST CHAD'S, SHREWSBURY: *The neglect of churches during the 17th and 18th centuries left many in a perilous state. Therefore, when a young engineer called Thomas Telford was asked to inspect the medieval St Chad's church in Shrewsbury, the congregation should not have been surprised when he told them it was about to collapse! They ignored his advice and while he went on to international fame, the church lasted barely six months before, as he had predicted, the tower fell down and destroyed the building! The new structure in a Neoclassical style was completed in 1792 and was one of a number with round naves from this period.*

FIG 4.15 NORTH RUNCTON, NORFOLK: *As with many churches in this period, they were only built when the old one had finally collapsed, as happened here when its predecessor's steeple fell down. The new building completed in 1713 has a square nave with a central projection with pediment above and a lantern on top of the tower.*

FIG 4.16 COWLINGE, SUFFOLK: *It is often only part of a church which was rebuilt in this period, as in this case where a new brick tower was built in 1733 at the west end of the medieval church.*

FIG 4.17 ALDGATE, LONDON: *St Botolph's was designed by George Dance and completed in 1744, with its inventive stacking of Classical details but less exuberant than Wren's earlier Baroque. As with many churches in this period, it is not aligned on an east-west axis but in this case runs north-south due to the road which it is built within.*

FIG 4.18 NEWCASTLE UPON TYNE:
*All Saints' church was designed by
David Stephenson and completed in 1796.
This Neoclassical church has an
elliptical nave (see Fig 4.14), a portico on
four columns across the entrance and
low segmental arched windows to
the sides which are characteristic of
this style.*

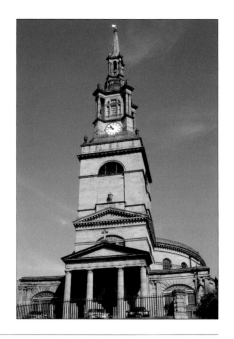

FIG 4.19 WITLEY COURT, WORCS: *A spectacular Rococco interior in white and
gold which dates from the mid-18th century. Georgian churches were always
spacious and light.*

CHAPTER 5

Victorian Churches
——————1830–1900——————

FIG 5.1 GRINDON, STAFFS: *The Victorians were enthusiastic revivalists and nowhere is this more clearly displayed than in their churches. This hilltop farming community in the Peak District had its small chapel replaced in 1845 by this larger church in a late 13th-century style with a spire copied from the East Midlands. Vernacular architecture had been replaced by materials and features from another place and time.*

It was only so long that the Church authorities could ignore the changes caused by a population shifting to the new industrial towns and cities. During the 1830s and 1840s they created new parishes to serve these urban congregations and with them came a wave of church building and restoration influenced by the Oxford Movement and the Cambridge

Camden Society. These sought a return to the earlier period of the Church of England with a more Catholic stance and insisted that Gothic was the appropriate form of architecture for a place of worship. In addition to this, the Catholic Emancipation Act of 1829 now permitted its long suppressed congregation to build their own places of worship in public and new churches were also erected for the 'old' religion.

In this unprecedented building boom, it was the professional architect rather than the master mason who oversaw all aspects of the design and, rather than be confined to the locality, he could now source materials and skills from further afield. This meant fine quality stone and brick which would not have been widely available to medieval masons could now be used on Victorian churches thanks to improved transportation, and with mass production many of the parts required were available immediately and at a cheaper price. The result was unified

FIG 5.2 ST MARY'S RC CHURCH, LEEK, STAFFS: *Many churches in this period were built for the newly emancipated Roman Catholic Church. This edifice dating from the 1880s has used the late 13th century for inspiration but mixes two different stones: the grey masonry rough hewn and the lighter smooth, a common mix in the mid to late Victorian period.*

FIG 5.3 EDENSOR, DERBYS: *There was also much change in the countryside as the last wave of enclosures and continued emparkment in the first half of the century resulted in the creation or reshaping of villages. Most of the houses in this view were built from 1838–42 as the owners of Chatsworth sought to move the old community out of sight of their house. The church was rebuilt in 1867 by George Gilbert Scott, the most famous of the Victorian church restorers.*

FIG 5.4: *Victorian and later restorers often stripped away centuries-old render or whitewash from walls, revealing a patchwork of stone and brick which the original builders had never intended to be exposed. The above example reveals numerous phases of stonework, as well as the old arcade arch filled in with brick and later still a modern window inserted. Note the right-angled grooves on some stones, reused from a previous structure.*

Gothic buildings erected in a matter of a few years rather than decades appearing in neat walled churchyards all over the country.

In many rural locations chapels of ease had long served remote farming communities, but now with many of these areas benefiting from industries like quarrying, mining and agriculture the buildings were upgraded to a church with its own parish and burial ground. This might have resulted in a complete new structure (as in Fig 5.1),

an enlarged nave, or just the addition of a feature like a tower.

Those churches which remained the centres of their parish were not immune from this wave of Gothic revival. Victorian restoration was essential as years of neglect had left many buildings in a ruinous condition and architects set about rebuilding the structure and stripping interiors to create what was then considered an appropriate style. Much of the work was centred on the chancel where vibrantly coloured stained glass replaced the clear, the reredos behind the altar was repaired or fitted, walls were painted, roofs filled with patterned panels and the floor covered with new encaustic tiles. In the process, however, they inadvertently destroyed much of the

FIG 5.5 LITTLEWORTH COMMON, MAIDENHEAD: *Many new churches were simple in design with a bellcote rather than a tower. The deeply carved stones, looking like they have been hewn out of the quarry, would never have appeared on medieval buildings but were popular in the late 19th century.*

FIG 5.6: *Despite the awakening of the Church of England to the changing times, dissenting groups were still influential and chapels were built in their thousands, from huge urban red brick structures to humble corrugated iron shacks, to serve more remote or poorer communities. Whatever the size, there is generally a single large body with a prominent and symmetrical main façade. The polychromatic mix of brickwork in this example was popular on all buildings in the 1860s and 1870s.*

medieval artwork they sought to imitate and often replaced it with structures of indifferent architectural quality, resulting in extreme derision from later critics.

By the turn of the 20th century there was a growing awareness of the value of the original medieval buildings and vigorous restoration became more sensitive preservation. New churches continued to be built, but they were more modest structures to meet the demands from rapidly expanding suburbs. The continuing shift of population and falling attendances during the middle of the last century have left many churches with a

congregation unable to support its hefty maintenance bill or in the worst cases the building has been abandoned. Church authorities, English Heritage, the National Trust and most notably charitable groups like the Redundant Churches Trust have been active in saving these icons of the community for future use.

Victorian Churches

The revival of Gothic architecture which came to dominate church building in this period did not just happen overnight. The pointed arch had been used in the late 18th century but these wide openings with 'Y'-shaped tracery (see Fig 4.11) were

FIG 5.7: *The above is one example of over 600 Commissioners or Waterloo Churches which were erected after the 1818 Church Building Act. They were built on the cheap but used a simplified Gothic style and stand as a link between the whimsical Revival of the late 18th century (see Fig 4.11) and the more accurate Victorian work to follow.*

FIG 5.8 ST GILES' (RC), CHEADLE, STAFFS: *One of Pugin's finest churches, completed in 1846 and accurately using the Decorated style throughout.*

distorted decorative features upon essentially Classical buildings and are termed Gothick to differentiate them from the more correct later versions. Leading architects were often more happy to work from medieval structures than they were from ones of Ancient Rome or Greece, and in the early 19th century, as clients became more aware of our nation's own past glories, so they demanded a more authentic Gothic style.

There had been little study made of this art form from the Middle Ages until an enthusiastic young architect, Augustus Welby Pugin, made it his life's work (unfortunately a very short life as he died from overwork at the age of 40). In addition to his designs with Charles Barry for the Houses of Parliament, he built a number of richly decorated and accurate Gothic structures for the newly emancipated Catholic Church, to which he later

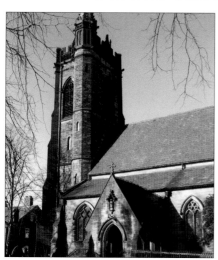

FIG 5.9: *The early Victorian Gothic churches tend to have very steep pitched roofs and to use the Decorated style for inspiration. Stained glass windows with rich blues were reintroduced in this period. Although these appear medieval at first glance, the use of the same style and material, and its similar condition throughout, indicates it is a Victorian church.*

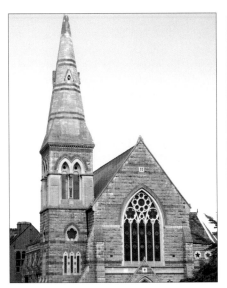

converted. His designs and writings were influential in reviving the pointed arch and making the medieval come back to life in amongst blackened factories and chimneys.

Later in the century the next generation of architects used the buildings of the past to inspire new forms rather than making direct copies and these are often crudely grouped together under the Arts and Crafts banner. Some structures appear to grow out of the landscape rather than dominating it (see Fig 5.16) while others are jumbled arrangements of vernacular materials and styles (Fig 5.14). The Gothic was still the dominant style, although by the turn of the century its features had been simplified; they looked medieval from a distance but have a distinctive modern appearance on closer inspection.

FIG 5.10: *Mid-Victorian Gothic churches often featured different colours of brick and stone and tend to use the Early English (pictured here) and Perpendicular as a source.*

FIG 5.11: *The Romanesque style inspired by Italian buildings was popular in the mid-Victorian period with round arched openings and a campanile rather than Gothic tower. This example by Arthur Blomfield was designed in 1869 and used concrete for part of its construction.*

FIG 5.12: *Arts and Crafts churches appear more humble, use local or rustic materials and have distinctive sloping buttresses and low mullion windows.*

FIG 5.13 EXEMPLAR CHURCH c1900: *The final visit to Exemplar church shows the village has grown into a small town with the church and manor house left stranded on its edge. Despite building new places of worship in town, the Victorians have restored the old church with a new chancel and upper stage of the tower. They have also stripped off the render to expose the various stages of stonework in its 900-year life.*

STILL OUT THERE

**FIG 5.14
BROCKHAMPTON-BY-
ROSS, HEREFORD:**
*Completed in 1902 by
W.R. Lethaby, this church
is Arts and Crafts at its
most inventive and
whimsical. Every material
and vernacular style has
been carefully arranged to
create a structure which at
first glance seems medieval
but upon closer inspection
uses new forms of
decoration in a calculated
arrangement (low mullion
windows are a favourite
Arts and Crafts feature).*

**FIG 5.15 STUDLEY ROYAL, NR
RIPON, WEST YORKS:** *Designed
by William Burges and completed
in 1878, this is a wonder of
Victorian Revivalism maintained
by English Heritage (part of the
National Trust's Fountains Abbey
site). It uses the 13th-century
Early English for inspiration, with
its spire and geometric tracery, but
details like the buttresses are
exaggerated and the composition
is too perfect to be of medieval
foundation. Wide segmental
arches, as over the entrance on the
west end of the tower, were
popular on Arts and Crafts
buildings.*

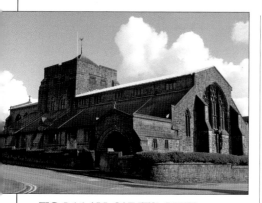

FIG 5.16 ALL SAINTS', LEEK, STAFFS: *This squat building was designed by the famous late Victorian architect Richard Norman Shaw in the 1880s and rather than just copy features from the past as on earlier Victorian churches, he has used these to inspire new forms (note the overly wide porch and mullion windows).*

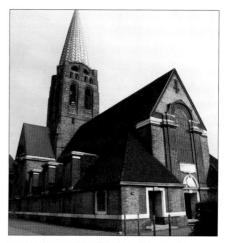

FIG 5.17 HAMPSTEAD GARDEN SUBURB, LONDON: *This development laid out in the early 1900s had two places of worship designed by Sir Edwin Lutyens as its centrepiece – a domed Roman Catholic church and this Anglican church with a spire.*

FIG 5.18 ST LUKE'S, CHELSEA, LONDON: *Everything was so easy to categorize up to this date and then the Revivalists had to mess it up by dipping into their box of historic garnish! This spectacular parish church is an early example based on a Perpendicular chapel (note the flying buttresses) with a tall, narrow tower and five-arched portico across the front (more typical of the early 19th century) The bands wrapped around the corners of the tower and the Wren-like pinnacles on top do not look medieval.*

**FIG 5.19
BROCKHAMPTON-
BY-ROSS,
HEREFORD:** *The nave
of W. R. Lethaby's
church (see Fig 5.14)
with steep pitched roof,
low eaves, plain walls
and excellent use of
light, typical of Arts
and Crafts interiors.*

**FIG 5.20 STUDLEY
ROYAL, NR RIPON,
WEST YORKS:** *One of
the finest and most
richly decorated of
Victorian chancels (see
Fig 5.15). After
centuries of
whitewashed walls the
19th century witnessed
a return in many
churches to the glories
of medieval colour (the
Victorians had a wider
pallet to choose from).*

SECTION II

THE
CHURCH
IN DETAIL

CHAPTER 6

The Nave

Aisles, Transepts, Roofs and Porches

FIG 6.1: *A drawing looking down the nave of a church towards the chancel at the east end with labels of some of the features you are likely to see.*

THE NAVE

The nave is the main body of the church, its name derived from *navis*, the Latin word for ship, and it is where the congregation would stand or sit during services. As it was for the public's use, it was generally considered their responsibility and the dating of principal building phases or lavish decoration can highlight affluent periods in the history of a parish.

The main entrance is usually by the south door but, in some, it is the north (which was used as an exit for processions in medieval times). To the west there is often a grand entrance used for special occasions, while the east end is usually divided off from the chancel by the arch and originally a screen (see Chapter 7). In the Middle Ages it was often the only large public space so it could have been used for manorial courts and fairs with stalls even erected within, while its design had to allow for the regular processions which would take place throughout the Christian calendar.

The nave is rectangular in plan with the exception of a few round ones dating from the Norman and the Georgian periods (also square and polygonal in the latter). The walls were very thick in Saxon and Norman buildings to counter the outwards thrust of the roof (see Fig 2.3), while later ones became thinner as deeper buttresses along the outer wall carried more of the load from above. The walls will usually have an outer and inner skin with rubble set in mortar in between. Timber scaffolding and hoists would have been used during construction with horizontal pieces set in the wall as it grew to hold the temporary structure firm. When it was removed upon completion the 'putlog holes' where the scaffolding was fixed were filled in with mortar but this often falls out later and the holes can be found today on the outer wall (especially towers).

Aisles

It was common in most churches for the nave to be expanded, especially in the 13th and 14th centuries when the population reached its medieval peak, with the addition of aisles, lean-to structures along the north and south walls. When this was done the old nave wall was broken through with new arches and columns (an arcade) inserted to support the original upper part, hence it is often this latter part which may be the oldest section in the building. Aisles built in the 12th and 13th century tend to be narrow while those built in the following centuries are usually wider although many earlier ones would have been enlarged. Later, if congregations dwindled, one or both might have been abandoned, with bricked-up arches or marks on the outside wall the clues to show where they once existed (see Fig 5.4).

The short part of the nave wall which stands above where the aisle roof butts up is called the clerestory. When aisles were added the windows were pushed further out, making the nave darker, so to cast more light a row of small openings could be inserted along this upper section of wall. Although these may have been fitted when the aisles were built, most date from the

FIG 6.2: *The nave was the part on which many rich locals chose to spend their money, fitting the latest flat pitched roof and lavish decoration, while the priest and church often exhibited less enthusiasm to maintain the chancel. It is common to see a grand nave in the later Perpendicular style but with an older chancel still having a steep pitched roof, as here at Great Horwood, Bucks.*

Perpendicular period when new flatter roofs replaced older steep pitched roofs (look for a triangular mark on the tower to show where this has happened). Either the new windows replaced earlier smaller ones or they were being inserted for the first time. In the largest Norman churches the side walls of the nave could be divided further into three with a row between the arcade below and clerestory above, called a triforium (see Fig 2.27).

Transepts

Larger churches could also benefit from the addition of transepts to the north and south of the tower which created a crucifix church plan. These were and still are used as chapels, with additional altars provided for the clergy or private individuals, and often contain family memorials and tombs (see Chapter 7). They were usually built in conjunction with a central tower (especially in the 12th and 13th centuries), their bulk in effect

FIG 6.3: *The nave progressively became lighter and more spacious from the heavy oppressive Saxon interiors (Fig 1.23) to the airy Perpendicular (Fig 3.21). This example illustrates one of the important changes, the addition of a clerestory. The arcades to each side are Early English with narrow pointed arches and characteristic double chamfers, but later the roof was raised and a set of windows inserted on either side to brighten the interior. Note the two sets of triangular marks on the wall of the tower in the back showing the line of earlier roofs and the original belfry openings now within the nave.*

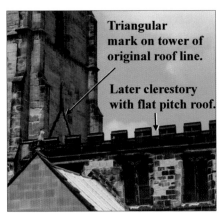

FIG 6.4: *A close up of the tower and the end of the nave where a clerestory and flatter roof have replaced an earlier steep pitched roof, the line of which is still visible above the battlements. Clerestories were very popular in eastern counties, less so in the far South-West.*

buttressing the structure, although sometimes this has either collapsed, been replaced by a west tower or one was planned but never built. The space under a central tower where the nave, transepts and chancel all met is called the crossing.

Roofs

The roof of the nave, as with the other parts of the building, was a crucial design feature and spanning such a large space in medieval times pushed masons' and carpenters' skills to the limit. In a few large churches the ceiling can be stone vaulted with the outer tiled or lead-covered roof above and a separate inner skin (the vault), which you see from inside with a hidden gap between the two. This vaulting was formed over temporary wooden centering erected within the church and its earliest form was simply a semi-circular covering known as a barrel or tunnel vault. Where two lengths met at right angles there was formed a diagonal cross shape. It was soon realized that if ribs were run along these joints, transferring the load down to the walls, then the vaulting between could be much thinner, making construction cheaper and easier (Fig 6.5.). This simplest form of rib vaulting which appeared in the Late Norman period was further elaborated upon over the centuries with additional, mainly decorative pieces in between to create complex patterns. The final most ambitious form was fan vaulting (Fig 3.12), with numerous ribs flowering from high in the wall and intricate stonework between forming its distinctive fan shape. Vaulting is rare in the nave of a church, except in old abbey churches which were adopted by the parish after the Dissolution; however, it can be found in smaller spaces like an aisle, chapel or in a porch.

Most parish churches have a wooden roof so you see the underside of the supporting timbers from inside the nave or an inserted ceiling hiding it from view. Steep pitched roofs were held in place by a series of trusses, triangular arrangements formed from two diagonal rafters with a horizontal beam either at the bottom (tie beam) or higher up (collar beam). Early examples often used a central vertical king post running up to the ridge piece or a shorter crown post as part of the structure.

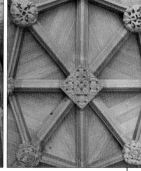

FIG 6.5: *A simple groin vault with ribs along a side aisle of an old priory church (left) and a close up of a later rib vault with diagonals linked by thinner liernes (right). The decorative bosses added at intersections were a weight designed to hold the ribs down and stop them from rising. In fan vaulting the ribs are not structural but carved out of slabs.*

FIG 6.6: *Later medieval types of roof which you are likely still to see today (some may be more modern replicas). Hammer beams were popular in the east of the country, arch braces and tie beams are generally more widespread. There is much regional variation and period detailing in roofing, of which these are but the crudest simplification.*

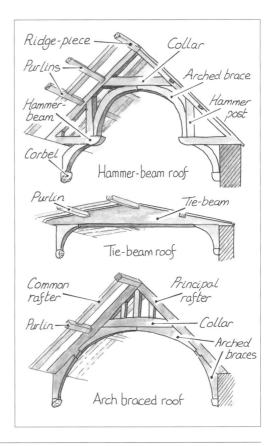

As most churches have been re-roofed since construction, they are more likely to have a later type which had prominent longitudinal purlins and common and principal rafters to form types known as double framed. These could either have a large tie beam with just its top edge or its whole length cambered to match the flat pitch of the covering, or an arched brace which curves to match a steeper one, both types being supported by stone brackets (corbels) below where they

FIG 6.7: *Tie-beam roofs with decorative stone corbels and wooden angels (left) and carved bosses (right).*

meet the wall. A hammer-beam roof is an ingenious arrangement in which a short horizontal timber projects out from the wall a short way and upon its end an arched brace springs up to a collar, permitting a larger width to be spanned without blocking the view to the east window.

These later roofs could be embellished with carved angels and decorative bosses, while the gaps between rafters could be boarded or plastered, sometimes just a short section over where the rood screen stood at the front of the chancel. A distinctive type popular in the West Country is the waggon roof, in which the gap between the underside of arched braces is panelled in to form the appearance from inside the church of the canvas covering of an old waggon.

Porch and Door

The porch which sheltered the main entrance into the nave (hence usually on the south side) was more than just somewhere to keep out of the rain. It was used as part of the baptism and marriage services. It was where local business deals could be sealed and notices pinned relating to manorial courts which could be held within the church. The door acted as a sanctuary for those evading the law by holding the ring upon it, a right which was not completely revoked until 1621.

The earliest types of porch tend to project only a short way off the wall and many churches either did not have one or just erected a simple timber structure which has since been replaced. By the 14th and 15th century they became a popular new addition, bequeathed to the church by a wealthy local and displaying lavish decoration, with sometimes a room above which was used by the clergy and also served as a school, armoury or a library in some cases.

The structure itself reflected contemporary style with the arched entrance and decoration datable from the details illustrated in previous chapters. Timber ones which were popular in the South-East are trickier to date and many were built or restored in the past few hundred years.

The doorway which it covers will often be older than the porch, and many have an elaborate Norman tympanum above from when the

FIG 6.8: *A Perpendicular two-storey porch with a small room above, which could have been used as accommodation for a priest, a school room or library, or for holding arms.*

FIG 6.9: *A late medieval door from Ashwell, Herts, which still has its fittings including a sanctuary ring on its outer face (left) and the grid of timber strengthening it on its inner face (right). In some there may still be a stoup on the right-hand side of the entrance which originally held holy water for worshippers to bless themselves with before entering.*

removed most traces of medieval decoration. The outside of the building could have been rendered and painted or whitewashed with window tracery picked out in bolder colours. Within the nave most of the wall surface would have been covered with images of saints and stories from the Bible, warning the illiterate congregation of what would happen to them if they blasphemed. Columns and capitals would have been painted, the ceiling and roof trusses too, often with decorative detail picked out in gilt. It was restoration mainly in the 20th century which has uncovered what remains of this and it is not unusual to find fragments left exposed in many churches.

The floor in most churches would

FIG 6.10: *It is common to find scratched marks around the entrance to a church. A small hole on the outer face with radiating lines is a scratch dial and originally a wooden stick would be set in the middle to act as a sundial, often with a deeper mark indicating the time for mass. Other markings include crosses carved by someone as proof of making a vow, mason's marks or even medieval graffiti.*

entrance was open to the elements (see Fig 1.9). The reassuringly heavy creaking door may itself be of antiquity with some decorative ironwork surviving from the 12th and 13th centuries (although the wood may have been renewed) and many more may be from the 14th and 15th centuries when it was fashionable to have it divided into long thin panels with tracery at the top.

THE NAVE IN DETAIL
Decoration
One of the most surprising aspects of churches is that they were originally a riot of colour. It was only in the hundred years after the Reformation that white-washing, neglect and destruction

FIG 6.12: *The interior of St Mary's, a small Norman church at Kempley, Glos, has one of the finest displays of medieval wall paintings including the wheel of life (left) and a doom (above the chancel arch). The latter was the most significant painting in a church and it formed a background to the great rood which originally hung or stood in front of it. Most had Christ showing his wounds with Hell on one side and Heaven on the other.*

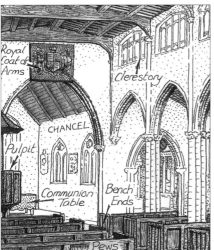

FIG 6.13: *St Agatha's church next to the remains of Easby Abbey, North Yorks, has wall paintings dating from the 13th century as in this example showing the Expulsion from the Garden. Other popular images in medieval churches were St George, St Margaret and St Catherine, and the seven deadly sins. St Christopher carrying Christ over the river was probably the most frequent and was often found opposite the main entrance.*

FIG 6.11: *The nave was a riot of colour, covered with wall paintings conveying messages to an illiterate congregation before the Reformation (top). By the late 17th century the same nave is whitewashed with a pulpit, pews and a Royal Coat of Arms in place of the doom (bottom).*

have originally been no more than beaten earth, usually hardened with a substance like animal's blood and then sprinkled over with rushes or grass (which would be regularly swept out and replaced). The finest may have had stone flags although these were usually fitted in more recent centuries. Medieval tiles were a luxury product reserved for the area around the altar and they would usually have a patterned surface finished in red and yellow. The Victorians copied these and when renovating or fitting heating pipes under the floor they covered the old surface with plain red tiles and patterned ones in the chancel. It is these later machine made tiles or stone flags that you will find in most churches today.

Fonts

The first feature you are likely to come across upon entering the nave is the font, the receptacle for holding holy water. This was considered of such value in the medieval period that most had a lockable cover to prevent theft, which sometimes could be tall, elaborately carved conical pieces raised and lowered by chains. Because of this importance and the fact it can be moved, the font is one item which was retained when the church was rebuilt and hence they are often of great antiquity.

There is great regional variation in the design of fonts but there are some general features which help date them in addition to the style of decoration (see Chapters 1–5). Just a few survive from the Saxon period but more than a thousand can be found from Norman times. These have large bowls (as baptism involved immersion of the whole baby at this date), are usually square or circular and

FIG 6.14: *A late Norman font with its characteristic large bowl (left), one from the early 14th century with cusped tracery and crockets as in Decorated churches at the time (centre) and a 15th-century example with coats of arms and square flowers distinctive of the Perpendicular style (right). Originally fonts would have been painted in bright colours like the interior of the church, and occasionally fragments can be found. Some medieval fonts were made from lead, but these have later been destroyed, some even used to make musket balls in the Civil War.*

FIG 6.15: *Another feature often found around the west end of the church is the parish chest, a lockable wooden type in which originally would have been kept valuables. Most had three locks with the vicar having one key and churchwardens the others. The earliest could simply be a roughly squared log with the top cut off to form a lid. The late medieval ones, which are still quite numerous, are made from slabs of wood bound together by ironwork; some from the 15th century have the short end extended down to raise it off the damp floor. This example from Whitby was stolen in the 18th century and thrown over the nearby cliffs and although it survived it was found empty.*

are often decorated with mystical beasts and figures. In the late 12th century some were produced with a chalice-shaped bowl raised on four columns in each corner (Fig 6.14, left). By the 14th century octagonal ones with niches and sometimes tracery patterns had become popular (Fig 6.14, centre). In the following century they were often set upon steps (though many have been raised up like this in more recent centuries).

Gallery

A raised floor of wooden seating supported on columns which first appeared in churches when the rood lofts, part of the screen across the chancel where musicians could play from, were destroyed after the Reformation. To replace them small galleries were inserted at the west end or within the tower from which they could play. Later, as the population grew, wooden galleries were inserted within the medieval nave, some just at the west end, others on all three sides facing the pulpit. These have often been stripped out in more recent times but

FIG 6.16: *Galleries were a popular addition, especially in the 18th century when extra seating was needed for a growing congregation. As in this example from Whitby, they were often clumsily inserted covering windows and drowning out the medieval features. Note the top of the triple-decker pulpit (right) with a sounding board above.*

are still common in Georgian churches and later chapels where they were part of the original structure.

Coat of Arms

A common feature in the nave is a large board hung on the wall (now often found above the south doorway) with a coat of arms painted upon it. One type is a hatchment, a diamond or lozenge-shaped frame usually with the word

FIG 6.17: *An example of a Royal Coat of Arms with the initials of Charles I dating it to 1625–49. The countries represented within the quarters also changed over time and can help dating. In the 17th century England was top left, the fleur-de-lys of France bottom right (or they share both quarters as above), with Scotland top right and the harp of Ireland bottom left. With the Union of England and Scotland in 1707 their arms share both the top left and bottom right quarters and then the dropping of the claim to the French throne meant from 1801 that England was in two and Scotland and Ireland the others.*

Resurgam below the coat of arms, meaning 'I will rise again'. These were boards which were hung for a couple of months in front of the house of the deceased and surviving examples usually date from the late 17th or early 18th centuries. Their layout and colour of background also identified the deceased's marital status.

The other type is the Royal Coat of Arms, which was originally hung above the chancel arch after the Reformation. They became common in Elizabeth I's reign but most surviving examples date from after the Restoration of the Monarchy in 1660 and then have usually been moved to a less prominent position in the Victorian period. They will normally have the initials of the monarch on them but they can also be dated from the subtle changes to the Royal Coat of Arms over the centuries. For instance, a gold lion in the centre, introduced by William of Orange, dates one painted between 1689 and 1702, and the white horse of Hanover in a similar position dates from the Georgian period. The Tudors also had the Welsh dragon as one of the supporters but this was changed to the familiar unicorn by James I. It was also common for an older coat of arms to be updated, so in the 18th century the initial of the king could be changed from a 'C' to a 'G' and the white horse simply added in the middle.

Benches and Pews

It was rare to find seating in the nave during the Middle Ages. Most stood or knelt during the service, which being held out of view behind the screen

FIG 6.19: *Box pews were a common addition in the 17th and 18th centuries, some just reserved for the wealthy, others more generally spread around the nave as in this example from York.*

FIG 6.18: *The boards at the end of the benches were often carved, some highly decoratively as in the above example. Poppy heads at the top were popular in East Anglia (derived from the figurehead of a ship, the 'puppis', and not the flower); square headed ones were the norm in Somerset, and linenfold patterns were carved in the centre of Tudor examples.*

permitted people to come and go without disturbing the clergy. A stone plinth was often provided around the wall for the elderly or infirm, from which we get the phrase 'gone to the wall'. In the late medieval period as the idea of a sermon being preached directly to the congregation gained importance so benches became more common, and then after the Reformation with the priest turning round to face them, seating became a standard fitting. At the same time the

loss of the chantry chapels meant the wealthy families wanted somewhere private to sit, so family pews were created (sometimes within the old chantry chapel). They could have a canopy above and some their own fireplace, while a convenient exit back to the manor house to avoid the rush to leave was essential!

Pulpits

As the sermon gained importance, a pulpit from which it could be preached would be provided and there are a small number of late medieval survivors in wood and stone, usually with a distinctive slender stem beneath. Far more survive from the early 17th century as they became a standard fitting and these have distinctive rich wooden carving with semi-circular

FIG 6.20: *A stone medieval pulpit with a slim stem (left) and a Jacobean pulpit (early 17th-century) with distinctive round arch decoration (right) both from Nantwich, Cheshire. Some still have a bracket fixed to them from which an hour glass was hung to regulate the time of the sermon.*

arched decoration and sometimes a sounding board above. In the late 17th and early 18th centuries a triple-decker with the pulpit, a lectern and prayer desk all in one was popular (see Fig 6.16).

The lectern was usually a freestanding piece originally sited in the chancel before being moved to the front of the nave after the Reformation. Some are wood, others brass, often with the top in the shape of an eagle with outstretched wings (the symbol of St John the Evangelist) and around 50 or 60 originals survive from the 15th and 16th centuries.

Stained Glass

No feature of the church is so immediately recognizable as stained glass windows and few can fail to be moved by their stunning displays of colour as the sun pours in behind them (it is more correct to call them painted glass). Most today are Victorian as

medieval ones were smashed out and replaced by clear glass in the century after the Reformation. A few early examples did survive and many others were refitted when the church was restored, albeit in a jumble of fragments set in a single opening (Fig 6.21).

Glass was a luxury during the medieval period and most early churches would have had shutters or oiled cloth across windows with tracery and leaded panes only becoming common in the late 13th century. The patterns were marked out on a board and pieces of coloured glass cut to fit with lead strips between holding them in place and wires attaching these to bars fixed into the window frame to prevent wind damage (Fig 6.21, bottom). These early types used rich reds and blues with yellow stain being introduced in the 14th century (figures of this date also have a slightly 'S'-shaped stance). Details like faces could be added by black stain and shading with tones of brown, both being fired to fix them to the glass.

The height of medieval stained glass came in the 15th century, with the rectangular panels created by the Perpendicular tracery giving a more convenient space for elaborate designs. Three-dimensional richly coloured pictures, often with heraldic symbols, were popular with the red, blue, green and yellows being broken up by clear white pieces. Victorian stained glass is distinctive because of this lack of clear glass, it seems darker with much use of blue and red, while the figures on closer inspection match those of contemporary paintings.

FIG 6.21: *Examples of medieval stained glass. These windows were destroyed in the years after the Reformation and have been restored but with some fragments which could not make a complete image inserted in an abstract manner, as can be seen in the detail above the figures in each picture. Note the horizontal support bar with rings of wire (bottom) which stop the glass from being blown out.*

FIG 6.22: *Most stained glass windows are Victorian (top) and tend to contain a lot of blue and red as opposed to medieval ones which used more clear glass (medieval glass tends to look silvery from the outside). Recent examples are usually more daring and like this example (right) use the window as a whole, ignoring the tracery divisions.*

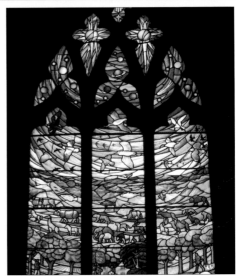

CHAPTER 7

The Chancel
Altars, Chapels and Memorials

Labels in figure: East window, Reredos, Wall tablet, Easter sepulchre, Niches, Piscina, Stalls, Sedilia, Altar rails, Misericord, Screen, Altar, Screen, Ledger (graveslab), Chest tomb

FIG 7.1: *Drawing showing the inside of a chancel with labels of some of the features you will find there.*

As the nave was the responsibility of the congregation, so the chancel was that of the clergy. It was the area in a medieval church where the service took place with the altar as its centrepiece and a rood screen at its west end enclosing it from view. This perpetuated the great mystery of the mass to the public back in the nave, enhanced further by it being chanted in Latin. As it was maintained by a priest who was often little better off than the congregation it usually relied upon the finances of the mother church or monastery for any building work. It is often the case that after its initial build the chancel would receive just enough for basic repairs and have a modest appearance compared with some of the splendours lavished by the public upon the nave, until the Victorians restored the balance.

Most Norman and occasionally Saxon churches originally had an apse (see Fig 1.22), typically a short semi-circular extension to the east end of the chancel, in which senior members of the clergy could sit during a service. In the same period there may have also been a crypt below the altar in which relics were housed, with a passage called an ambulatory around the outside for pilgrims to access or view them.

By the 13th century the altar had moved closer to the east wall and the clergy and officials now sat to the side of it while the priest had his back to the nave during services. The chancel now became square ended (although those founded by the Celtic church had long been so) with a decorative altarpiece on the east wall. Additional altars were provided for relics, private individuals or guilds either at the east end of aisles or in purpose-built chapels to the side of the chancel. In the 14th and 15th

FIG 7.2: *The Saxon crypt at Repton, Derbys, dating from the 8th century (rebuilt in the 9th), under the chancel in which the remains of nobles and relics would have been housed. Such was the demand to see these venerated remnants or artifacts that many of the latter were manufactured until the authorities curbed the practice in the 13th century. Pilgrimages to visit these holy sites were huge undertakings and reached a fever pitch from the 12th to 14th centuries, such that relics were placed in side chapels to avoid disruption to services.*

FIG 7.3: *In many churches a section at the east end of an aisle or an additional building to the side (as here at St Mary's, Warwick) was provided to form a chantry chapel in which mass was chanted to the memory of the deceased who had paid for it. Sometimes the endowment left was not sufficient to cover a full permanent chantry due to inflation especially after the Black Death, so either they got a reduced amount of chanting or it stopped altogether.*

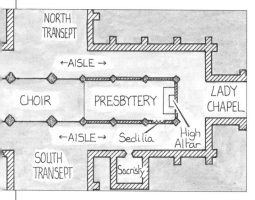

FIG 7.4: *In some of the largest churches (and cathedrals and abbeys) the layout of the chancel was more elaborate with a choir extending west under a crossing tower (where there was one) and a sanctuary containing the altar and a reredos (wooden or stone decorative screen). The aisles (often referred to as an ambulatory) ran around the outer edge of this area with side chapels leading off it and often an altar dedicated to the Virgin Mary at the east end (this area is then referred to as the Lady Chapel).*

provided in place of stone altars, walls were whitewashed and windows filled with clear glass. It was the Victorians who concentrated much of their restorative energies upon returning the chancel to their interpretation of its former glory, rebuilding the structure and decorating it with the rich colours we so often see today (see Fig 5.20).

centuries these were frequently built by wealthy locals who would pay for the building and for a priest to chant mass to his memory and are hence known as chantry chapels. Those dedicated to the Virgin Mary are referred to as Lady Chapels (see Fig 3.14).

With the Reformation this all changed. The new Church created under Henry VIII had an English Bible with the priest conducting services from a pulpit. Over the following century the rood screens were removed, new wooden communion tables were

FIG 7.5: *A rectangular opening at an angle through a wall is called a squint, which allowed someone from the side of the chancel arch or transept to watch the service behind the screen. It was often used by the person who had to ring the Sanctus bell at various points during the service, and these can sometimes be seen on the roof above the east end of the nave (see Fig 3.17). Squints will line up with the altar (as in this example from Burford, Oxon) and can be interesting where they don't, as this implies the chancel has been later extended and the altar re-sited further east.*

Chancel Arch and Rood Screens

The division between the nave and chancel is marked by the chancel arch and where they still survive (or replicas were installed) by the rood screen. The arch carries the load of the wall between the two parts and the size of the opening grew over time as technology permitted. Saxon ones tend to be narrow (see Fig 1.23), the Normans were more adventurous with the semi-circular arch, enhancing it with bands of decoration (see Fig 1.24), while later the pointed arch permitted it to become larger with the attention focusing more upon the screen below (see Fig 3.21).

The rood screen was a wooden or occasionally stone wall with a central opening or door over which was suspended a large crucifix (the rood).

The finest were brightly painted with tracery or cusps in the pointed arched openings and decorated panels below, some with a loft along the top from which musicians could play (the steps up to this in the wall often survive when the screen does not). Others were simpler in design, especially away from the rich wool areas, either running just across the end of the nave or in the South-West over the end of the aisles as well.

Above this, resting on the loft or a separate beam, was the great rood, a large crucifix with carvings of St Mary and St John either side. Some were of

FIG 7.7: *In Devon and other parts of the South-West the rood screen continued as one whole piece across the nave and aisles as here at Stoke in Hartland. In some churches, especially those off the beaten track, many of the medieval features survived, either missed by commissioners or saved by more sympathetic clergy.*

FIG 7.6: *A 15th-century painted screen from Felmersham, Beds showing some of the bright colours in which it, along with most of the interior, would have been painted before the Reformation.*

such size that they covered part of the doom painting above the chancel arch and the gaps where they once stood can still be found on the wall. A canopy of honour or rood celure was a section of the nave ceiling above this, which was decorated to highlight its importance. The rood was one of the first parts to go after the Reformation and as the interior was opened out for the new services the screen often followed suit. The doom was then whitewashed and a Royal Coat of Arms, Ten Commandments or Lord's Prayer was painted or hung over it.

Stalls and Misericords

Directly behind the screen in many larger or collegiate churches would have been wooden stalls, a single or double row either side. Medieval ones were built for members of the clergy and patrons and had flip-down seats with a projection on their underside called a misericord. This allowed the

person standing in front to rest during long services and most were decorated with symbolic or satirical carvings. The modern use of these stalls for choirs was introduced by the Victorians and they either reused existing ones or built new, copying original work to such a degree that the difference is hard to tell apart from general wear and tear.

Music was an important element in the medieval church and by the end of the period most had some form of simple organ, often positioned on the rood loft. A Sanctus bell was a small

FIG 7.9: *Misericords are wonderful details to study as they are one of the rare places where the medieval craftsman was free to express himself. Figures carved include birds, beasts and fishes, and themes like mythology, medieval romances (Reynard the fox was popular), domestic life and sports are frequently found. Fictional characters, monks, doctors and musicians, were also satirised. Considering the importance of those who rested upon them, it is surprising that sacred subjects are rare.*

FIG 7.8: *A detail of stalls from the collegiate church at Tong, Shropshire.*

hand-held type which was rung at set points during mass; the person doing so might have been sitting in the nave or transept so a squint may have been cut so he could see what was going on at the altar (see Fig 7.5). Some were also hung on the roof above the east end of the nave (see Fig 3.17). Puritanical dislike for joy in services meant most instruments were removed and the organ only began to reappear in the chancel after the Restoration, notably in Wren's churches, with those in use today mainly dating from the Victorian or modern period.

Piscina and Sedilia

Adjacent to the altar in a medieval church was a small stone basin, usually set in the south wall, called a piscina (Latin for basin or fishpond). This was used for washing the sacred vessels after the service and drained into the consecrated ground outside. Those fitted in Edward I's reign, 1272–1307, tend to have two bowls, the additional one for pouring down the ablutions from the chalice. Piscina found outside of the chancel can indicate where an additional altar was in medieval times.

Usually found next to this is a sedilia (from *sedile*, the Latin for seat), a set of three seats built into the south wall often with a decorated canopy above in the contemporary style. The priest would have sat on the eastern seat (often signified by being higher) while his deacon and sub deacon would sit on the others during the parts of the service which were sung.

FIG 7.10: *A piscina with an aumbry (recessed cupboard) used for storing cruets, i.e. jugs containing water and wine used in the services, and a small bowl for washing the priest's fingers. Some of the early piscina were supported upon a stone bracket or rested on a column as in this example, while others were built as part of the sedilia (see Fig 7.11).*

On the north side there is sometimes a wooden sanctuary chair used for visiting bishops. There may also be an Easter sepulchre where the Blessed Sacrament was placed from Good Friday to the Sunday. Most were temporary but a few stone ones survive, usually from the 14th century. Rectangular holes in the wall of the chancel are old aumbries, medieval cupboards which originally had doors

FIG 7.12: *An elaborate Easter sepulchre from Heckington, Lincs.*

FIG 7.11: *A sedilia with its characteristic three openings and a smaller piscina to the left. These examples were built with the seats on the same level, others may have them stepped. The canopy and decoration around sedilia and piscinas can help date them, ogee arches with cusps below and crockets above mean these examples are probably from the 15th century.*

across the front and contained the altar plate.

In most medieval churches the priest would come into the church via his own door to the side of the chancel, ready dressed and with all the components required for the service present. In the largest churches a separate sacristy may have been built in which vestments and vessels would have been stored with a private altar for the priest. In the Church of England

these side rooms are referred to as a vestry and most either were built in the Victorian period or were converted from pre-Reformation chantry chapels. Where these do not exist today, the vicar has to make do with a curtained-off part of the aisle or under the tower!

Altars, Communion Table and Reredos

The high altar (to differentiate it from the others which were sited in side chapels) was the centre point of the church, being the place where holy relics were originally contained. Medieval stone types had a slab on top (the mensa) with four crosses in each corner and a fifth in the middle and this part may survive even when the base below is of a later date. The roof above may have been decorated to emphasise its importance, sometimes with hooks

some a more elaborate reredos, a larger screen in stone (alabaster was popular in the medieval period and white marble in the Victorian) or wood was fitted with carved figures (these are usually modern replacements for those removed after the Reformation). To the front of the altar a railing runs from one side of the chancel to the other. These altar rails began to be fitted after the Reformation when it was found that without the rood screen the altar was too open and even dogs had to be kept out. Many rails date from the Jacobean period when they were fixed to discourage Puritans from moving the altar west into the body of the church.

FIG 7.13: *The chancel of St Botolph's church, Boston, Lincs, with its reredos dating from the 1890s running the full width of the wall. Where they are older, the statues are usually Victorian replacements for the originals destroyed after the Reformation. Above is the east window, usually the most impressive in the building. Some have niches either side, with the one on the north side usually for the patron saint of the church.*

in the ceiling from where Lent veils would have been hung. After the Reformation, communion tables were provided, many from the late 16th and early 17th century with distinctive bulbous legs.

In most medieval churches, on the wall under the east window would have been an altarpiece, a painting either directly on the wall or on panels. In

Internal Memorials

One of the aspects which brings a church to life is the memorials to the dead. Their names, ambitions, standing in society, even humour, can speak to us hundreds of years on through the design and epitaph on their grave slabs, wall plaques and tombs. Although many can be found within the nave it was the chancel, and more precisely the altar, which people would vie with each other to get closest to and it was only the wealthiest and most important members of the community who would be interred here.

Most memorials you find inside a church today will date from the 18th century when the middle classes clamoured to join the ranks of their superiors. This did not end until, due to the obvious health risk and unpleasant odour from having decomposing bodies a few inches from where daily services were held, legislation to ban internal burials was passed in the 1840s. The well off in the parish now had to be buried outside, either in the churchyard or in the new urban cemeteries where they had a free rein to build themselves spectacular tombs to display their standing in society.

Tombs

The Saxons rarely approved internal burials and in the 11th and even 12th centuries it was usually only the clergy who were permitted to be buried in the church. This would have been in a stone coffin set in the floor with a grave slab over it, but would have been a temporary resting place as the body was removed after a short while to a charnel house (a room, underground chamber or small

FIG 7.15: *Medieval stone coffins from Bakewell, Derbys. These are more correctly termed a sarcophagus as they had a hole in the bottom for the fluids from the decomposing body to escape.*

FIG 7.14: *Medieval grave slabs from Bakewell, Derbys. Earlier types tend to have a simple cross on top while on later ones they become more decorative with a stepped base as in these examples. There are no inscriptions as they were reused for other burials.*

building outside) and the coffin reused for someone else.

During the late 13th century permanent memorials to members of the wealthy local families began to appear in the form of tombs, a grave slab raised on a tall plinth with an effigy laid upon the top. The earliest effigies were roughly carved in wood or stone and covered in gesso (a chalky paste-like plaster of paris) in which was shaped the body's details. They were not representations of the deceased as accurate portraiture only developed in the 14th century. By this time stone and especially alabaster (a soft marble-like material, often with an orange or red vein) were used for the complete carving, with the whole piece then painted (fragments of this can still be

FIG 7.16: *A tomb with an alabaster effigy dating from the 15th century in Ashbourne church, Derbys. The pose of the effigy changed through time and along with the fashionable clothing and armour can help date these memorials. Knights with their hand upon their sword looking like they are ready to leap into action were popular from the late 13th to mid 14th century, then lying flat on their back with arms crossed until the turn of the 15th century when the hands were placed together in prayer and fashionable clothing as well as armour was common. It was also usual from this date for them to be shown next to an effigy of their wife, as in this example.*

FIG 7.17: *A 15th-century canopied tomb. The shape of the arch and the decoration around it as well as the style of the effigy can help date these. By the time this example was carved it was common to have shields with coats of arms along the sides of the tomb.*

FIG 7.18: *An alarming sight to modern eyes is a type of tomb which developed after the Black Death and through into the 16th century in which the space below the effigy was hollow and through its open sides can be seen the carving of a skeleton (cadaver), a humbling realization by the rich that they shared the same fate as the poor.*

found if you look closely on some tombs). These could either be on a freestanding tomb in the chancel or in a family chapel to one side, while some were recessed into the wall of the church with a canopy above.

Brasses

If you could not afford such a splendid memorial then a large brass plate set into a slab in the floor was the next best thing. Popular with the lesser gentry, merchants and professional classes, especially in the eastern counties, they were an alloy of tin and copper called latten (but known now as brass) and were cut into an impression of the profile of the deceased and an epitaph engraved.

The earliest date from the late 13th century when they tend to be large with deeply cut engraving, figures often in chain armour, with hair which curled up at the ends, some knights having crossed legs and the text in French. Examples from the late 14th and 15th

centuries wear contemporary clothing or plate armour, their hair usually straight (as in Fig 7.19), and the text in Latin and only later in English (the medieval clergy always used Latin on their memorials). The size gets smaller towards the end of the medieval period and the quality of engraving drops with heavily shadowed stiff figures. Despite this it remained a popular form of memorial into the later Tudor period although many of these may have been reused with an earlier engraving on the rear.

FIG 7.19: *Brasses are a useful source of information about the late medieval period as text is lacking or has worn away on other forms of memorial. Only a fraction of the original number survive as they were often ripped up around the time of the Civil War but the stone with the recess where they once were fixed is still clear in the floor of many churches.*

Monuments, Wall Plaques and Tombs

In the wake of the Reformation the wealthy directed their money away from the church, with the exception of memorials which could become monumental in size. In the later 16th and early 17th centuries some took the form either of a freestanding chest tomb with weepers (figures carved crying for the deceased) or coats of arms around the edge. Some were set onto a wall with husband and wife kneeling, while facing each other, and their children beneath them in a similar pose (those holding a skull having died before their parents). Others are rather flash figures resting their heads upon an elbow and dressed in the latest fashions.

From the late 17th century figures are increasingly found standing in classical dress, some even going to the extent of posing as Roman emperors. These reached a peak in the 18th century when white and black marble monuments (the painting of memorials in bright colours ends around this time), with huge figures dressed in robes and wigs and classical details on the front, dominated even the most humble country church.

Now farmers and professionals vied with the gentry and merchants to try and get buried within the building, usually with a wall plaque or a ledger, an inscribed stone slab set into the floor. In many churches the walls and floors became overwhelmed by memorials and the Victorians not only brought the practice to an end but also removed them as part of restoration.

FIG 7.21: *A rather ostentatious monument dating from the mid-18th century with the deceased dressed as a Roman emperor on the left of the Norman arch and a more subdued wall plaque of Greek inspiration from the early 19th century.*

FIG 7.20: *An early 17th-century tomb from Ashbourne, Derbys. As well as contemporary dress, fashionable architectural details can help date the memorials where dates are illegible. Here the geometric patterns up the sides, formed out of flat bands called strapwork, tend to date from the 1580s to 1620s.*

FIG 7.22: *An 18th-century wall memorial which must have been disturbing for the congregation, with such a stern figure staring down at them during services!*

CHAPTER 8

Towers and Spires

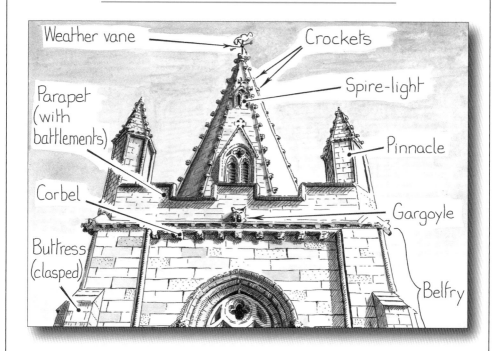

FIG 8.1: *A drawing of a tower, with a parapet spire and labels of some of the key features.*

The crowning glory of most parish churches is its tower or spire. It is a beacon visible from miles around which seemingly pins the village or town into the landscape. Yet it is the one part of the building which serves no ceremonial or liturgical purpose, its only role was to hold the bells and this had been done previously in freestanding wooden frames in the churchyard, making the tower really just an architectural luxury.

It was often the case that a village or wealthy individual tried to outdo their neighbour by adding a taller or more elaborate tower, this competition along with the properties of local materials and the limited area in which the masons worked helped create their distinct regionalization. The tall elaborate towers of Somerset and the spires of the East Midlands are just a couple of examples of these vernacular forms, a neat pattern which the Victorians displaced by importing their favourite types into virtually every area!

Despite this, 19th-century architects should be credited with saving many towers. As much as we can rightly marvel at the medieval builder who erected huge structures with simple tools, wooden scaffolding and experience rather than science, many did fall down, usually through poor

FIG 8.3 BYLAUGH, NORFOLK: *The most regional distinctive types of tower are the round ones of East Anglia. Most of the hundred or so which stand were built in the Saxon or Norman period, possibly with defence from raiders in mind. They may have served as a look out and had a ladder to get villagers in if under attack. On the other hand the lack of good building stone in the area made this form with no corners a more practical shape to build. This example has a 14th-century octagonal belfry section.*

FIG 8.2 BOSTON, LINCS: *Although a tower's principal purpose was to hold the bells, with the occasional use as a strong-room, refuge or beacon, the main motive was probably pride. The tallest medieval tower in England, the 288 ft Boston Stump, pictured here, may have been a feature useful to shipping coming into this busy port but it is more a demonstration of the wealth which this trade created for the town.*

foundation or later neglect (see Fig 4.14). What you see today might be an ambitious project which ran out of money and was capped off, a short tower which was heightened later or one which was in such a poor state that it was rebuilt, with only a lower portion surviving from its previous incarnation.

Early Towers

Towers were rare on parish churches before the 13th century and those which were built indicate that the building was a minster or in an important centre (Barton-upon-Humber in Fig 8.4, for instance, was a major port at the time). Some were narrow in form (see Fig 8.5), others broad when they were possibly used as a nave (see Fig 8.4 and 8.6).

FIG 8.4 BARTON-UPON-HUMBER, LINCS: *This notable Saxon tower dates from the late 10th century with similar triangular and round arched openings with vertical strips to Earls Barton (see Fig 1.20). When built the square base of the tower acted as the nave, with the small room to the left in this picture possibly used for baptisms and a similar one to the right being the chancel. This latter part was rebuilt around the time of the Norman Conquest and the tower heightened (the different masonry in the top section), then later still the present nave and chancel developed.*

Labels on Fig 8.4:
- 11th-century upper stage
- 10th-century tower
- 10th-century baptistry or porticus
- Nave, 13th century and later

FIG 8.5: *A distinctive narrow tower (left) from a 7th-century monastic church at Monkwearmouth (upper parts are later Saxon) and one dating from the 11th century from Marton, Lincs (right). Note the top of a blocked door on the latter just above the roof of the nave, a distinctive feature of Saxon towers, which was originally inside the nave – you can see the old roof line above it.*

FIG 8.6 FINGEST, BUCKS: *A large Norman tower with its distinctive belfry openings and bulky form, which dominates this tiny hamlet. It may have served as the nave on the original church as at Barton (Fig 8.4) though in similar towers the room at the bottom might have been used for accommodation for the priest. Above is a twin saddleback roof, a common late 17th- and early 18th-century method of covering large spaces. Originally it probably had a low pyramidal roof.*

FIG 8.7 KEMPLEY, GLOS: *A distinctive squat, plain Norman tower with a low pyramidal roof (details like the buttresses are later). Many 12th-century towers and some later had corbel shelves around the top (see Fig 1.13).*

The Normans built towers of similar form but with larger openings or erected central towers (with or without transepts) capped off by a low pyramidal roof (usually later replaced). The latter had the advantage that an elaborate west front and windows could be added, making a grand ceremonial entrance. These were probably built by a select few masons or churchmen and hence are similar in style, with little regional variation at this stage. They could also take a long time to build so the decoration could change the further up it reached.

Spires: Early English and Decorated

In the 13th and early 14th centuries the spire was the must-have addition for churches with a wealthy benefactor. Nobody knows its exact origins but it probably evolved by raising the pitch of the pyramidal roofs used on Norman

FIG 8.8 BARNACK, CAMBS: *This 13th-century rather squat spire is possibly the earliest surviving one in the country. It stands on top of a Saxon structure (note the rough masonry and vertical strips) and has pinnacles in the corners covering the junction between the octagonal bell stage and square tower.*

FIG 8.9 KIRBY BELLARS, LEICS: *A broach spire and tower dating from the late 13th and 14th centuries. The style and size of the spire lights can help date the structure.*

FIG 8.10 TREBETHERICK, CORNWALL: *This rather weather-worn broach spire dating from the 13th century slightly leans towards the top. This distortion and twisting is more common on lead-covered timber spires, as famously at Chesterfield, Derbys, which was probably caused by constant heating and cooling or unseasoned timber.*

towers as it better suited the new narrow lancet windows.

At the same time it was realized that an octagonal form was more appropriate for a spire, leaving a gap in each corner where it met the square top of the tower. Some of the earliest from the 13th century around Oxford resolved this by building pinnacles over these corners, but in the East Midlands small sloping triangular pieces called broaches were used, hence making the distinctive broach spire. It was also appreciated that ventilation was important to prevent damp so decorative openings shaped as windows with a triangular gable called spire-

lights were fitted, early ones tending to be large, subsequent ones smaller.

Later in the period, spires become taller often with decorative bands or crockets (small projecting leaf-like spurs) up the vertical angles. The most notable change was the addition of a parapet around the top of the tower, with gargoyles helping to drain the water off and the spire set behind and hence appearing finer. This had the advantage that ladders could be set on the tower making construction and maintenance easier.

FIG 8.11: *A splay footed wooden-shingle covered spire from Greensted, Essex (top), popular in the south where suitable stone was limited. Spikes are a distinctive feature of Essex, as with this example from Stansted Mountfitchet (centre). Some towers had a lean-to aisle wrapped around to cover part of the supporting timber work as here at Marton, Cheshire (bottom).*

FIG 8.12 ASTBURY, CHESHIRE: *A 14th-century parapet spire with a distinctive needle-like appearance. The parapets here are plain, but most would have had battlements. This is also an example of a detached tower, which is often due to poor foundations at the west end of the nave where most towers are sited.*

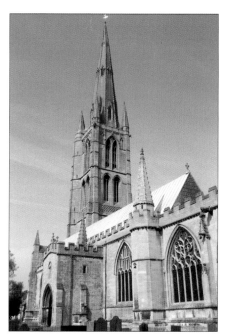

FIG 8.14: *The finest collection of Perpendicular towers is in Somerset, an area which grew rich at the time through the wool trade with individuals ploughing their personal wealth into these soaring spectacles. These examples from Backwell (left) and Winscombe (right) have the distinctive large belfry openings, elaborate parapets and pinnacles, and prominent buttresses (stepped back at Backwell and on the angle at Winscombe).*

FIG 8.13 GRANTHAM, LINCS: *One of the finest English church spires from the 14th century, with crockets down the corners (these form steps for steeplejacks). The optical effect of vertical features like columns appearing to bulge in the middle was countered in some spires by enlarging the crockets in the centre section (called entasis).*

Perpendicular Towers

In the late 14th century spires began to fall from fashion partly as the new Perpendicular style with broader, flatter arches and roofs better suited a squared-off tower rather than a fine point. Up until the Reformation thousands of new towers were built, some upon existing churches where there had been none or replacing an

FIG 8.15 YOULGREAVE, DERBYS: *Large Perpendicular towers are instantly recognizable by their height, prominent stepped buttresses, and large belfry openings with contemporary tracery. They also tend to have pinnacles and battlements around the top.*

FIG 8.16 GEDNEY, LINCS: *An example of a tower heightened in the Perpendicular period. The Early English structure below (note the original blocked belfry openings and the flat buttresses with columns up the corners) had an upper stage added with distinctive ogee arches and belfry tracery. The top appears blunt because a spire was planned but never completed and a small lead-covered spirelet stands in its place today.*

FIG 8.17 LITTLE MISSENDEN, BUCKS: *More humble Perpendicular towers are still distinguished by prominent buttresses, battlements and square-headed, cusped belfry openings. This example has a prominent stair turret, a feature popular in certain regions. Other staircases were hidden in corners or buttresses; just look for a series of narrow windows to see where they are.*

earlier central type, others as part of new ambitious projects. Most were taller than before with thinner but more prominent stepped buttresses in the corners and larger belfry openings in the style of the latest window tracery. The tops usually featured battlements or a parapet with decorative cut outs, often with pinnacles in the corners.

Later Towers and Spires

This great age of tower building came to an end with the Reformation, the great sums of money required for these symbols of local pride now being directed into private projects. Those which were built were increasingly made from brick, at first in the south and eastern counties but spreading out into the Midlands during the 17th century. After the Restoration in 1660 they began to reflect the new Classical styles, most notably on Wren's London churches (see Fig 4.3), although most were less ambitious with round arched belfry openings and a cupola or similar feature on the roof.

The Victorian love of the Gothic meant a return of the spire and it

FIG 8.18 BANGOR-IS-Y-COED, NR WREXHAM: *Georgian towers are distinguished by the use of Classical details upon a largely plain un-buttressed body. They also have round arched and circular openings and features like urns and cupolas on the top.*

FIG 8.19 FOSDYKE, LINCS: *A distinctive Victorian redbrick church with a tower capped off by a lead-covered spire. This material had been used on similar timber structures for centuries but copper, which turns green on exposure, was only used from the 18th century.*

became a prominent feature once again on the skyline of towns and cities. They were, however, generally copies of medieval types (see Fig 2.4) with little new invention. It was only later in the period and into the 20th century when squat Norman and tall Perpendicular towers were the inspiration, that new types appeared with simplified bold features. On those many churches built in this period for smaller communities, a bellcote had to suffice; a simple gabled top with a couple of openings housing the bells (see Fig 5.5).

Bells

The only practical reason behind the building of a tower was to house bells and more than 5,000 have a ring of five or more (usually only in the Church of England), sounding out a summons to services as well as alarms, celebration or tragedy. The oldest which can be accurately dated are from the 13th century, these medieval types tending to be narrower than later ones and they

FIG 8.20 HEDSOR, BUCKS: *Many churches in the 19th century had a simple bellcote added or a small bell turret as here on this late medieval flint and brick church.*

FIG 8.21: *Text on the upper band of a bell recording the date and, in the small box, that 'Henry Neale made mee'.*

are often inscribed with prayers. Most bells will date from after the Reformation, with inscriptions in English and the foundry's name upon them. The distinctive change ringing, when bells are rung one after another but with the order changing each time, was only introduced in the mid-17th century and is unique to this country.

The ringing starts with the bells in an upright position. As the rope attached to the wheel at the side of each bell is released their momentum enables them to complete a roughly 300° turn, which is stopped by stays fixed to the headstock hitting a slider below. As it swings, the clapper inside hits the

Wheel   Stays   Headstock

Slider   Frame

FIG 8.22: *A ring of bells with wheels set in a modern metal frame.*

sound bow (the thick metal rim at the mouth of the bell), the tone of the ring depending on the size and form of the bell.

Clocks

Although the congregation could be summoned by bells, the time for services could also be calculated by small scratch sundials upon the south side of the church (see Fig 6.10). Clocks did not appear on village churches until the 17th century with most dating to later. These early clocks could be most elaborate, with colourfully-decorated figures ringing bells or with elaborately projecting faces.

Weather Vanes

Telling the direction of the wind was important in a country which was dominated by agricultural concerns. The weather vane on top of the church tower has been a feature even included on the Bayeaux Tapestry and subjects on them include the cock, which symbolized vigilance, as well as dragons and fish.

CHAPTER 9

The Churchyard
Crosses and Memorials

FIG 9.1: *Haunting, peaceful and mysterious, the churchyard with its irregular display of tilting, ivy-clad gravestones is as memorable as the church which stands roughly in the centre of it. Some could have been used for over a thousand years and contain ten times as many graves, such a displacement of soil that the area can be many feet higher than the surrounding land! Over such a time they have also changed their appearance and use and their present form is in many cases a relatively modern creation.*

Mystery and superstition surrounds the origins of God's Acre. Some churchyards are certainly of ancient foundation – the presence of prehistoric stones and burial mounds on a number of sites shows that they have been sacred for thousands of years and that the Christian Church is just the latest incumbent. Some of these plots have a circular plan although this shape is not conclusive proof that it was either established in prehistory or by the early Celtic converts.

The first mention of a churchyard distinct from just a cemetery was not made until the late 8th century and probably contained a minster or church, a large cross and a graveyard,

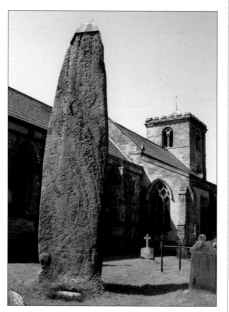

FIG 9.2 RUDSTON, YORKS: *This huge monolithic stone dates from prehistory and retained such sacred value that later the church was built alongside. The churchyard is also of a roughly circular plan which it shares in common with many other early sites. Another notable example is at Taplow, Berks, where an ancient burial mound within the graveyard was opened, revealing one of the richest early Saxon graves in the country.*

the boundary of which was originally marked out by small wooden crosses. Many churchyards may have been founded before a permanent building was erected, and would have contained just a wooden or stone preaching cross and perhaps the grave of a local dignitary or founding missionary which attracted further burials around it (see Fig 9.3).

Throughout the Middle Ages the churchyard was a communal area and, although revered, it served a function more than just a burial ground. In many places it was the only large public space so was used for fairs, plays, sports and celebrations, usually with a religious connection. Stalls were pitched in the grounds or in the church itself and on some urban sites permanent shops were built along the edge of the churchyard by a clergy never afraid to seize a business opportunity. There would have been a number of structures within the grounds, which could include a priest's house for the incumbent to live, a charnel house (or ossuary) in which bones from old graves were deposited, and a timber cage which would hold the bells at ground level before a tower for them became common.

The profusion of trees that characterize most churchyards today are generally an 18th- and 19th-century fashion; in the medieval period they would have appeared more open. Yews could have been found, some perhaps used as a grave marker. Willows or brambles were planted by families wishing to protect the resting place of loved ones from grazing animals kept

FIG 9.3: *The most notable remnants from Saxon churchyards are stone crosses, as in these examples from Bakewell, Derbys (left), Sandbach, Cheshire (centre) and Leek, Staffs (right). The largest are most likely to have been preaching crosses, consecrating the ground and marking the site for daily worship, in some cases probably before a church was erected. Other smaller stone crosses and slabs possibly marked an important grave. Some are bursting with carvings of scenes from the Bible, designed to educate the illiterate masses as medieval wall paintings in churches would later do (centre), others are much worn with limited decoration (right). Many Saxon crosses were destroyed in the hundred years after the Reformation, while their parts eroded over time, so that today most only survive in sections and are probably not in their original location.*

there by the priest, a problem which seems to have been more widespread after the Reformation and included the occasional building for animals on this hallowed ground. The most notable difference, though, would have been the lack of gravestones as the few who could afford a mason chose to be buried inside the church. It is likely that there would have been a large cross and then just an open area of hummocks, only broken up by a few small wooden markers or larger grave-boards on the more recent burials, which would quickly rot away.

By the 18th century the churchyard began to take on its more familiar modern appearance; trees were deliberately planted around the outer edge and topiary became popular. Boundary walls and fences replaced earlier ditches and banks, sometimes with the names of parishioners who paid for a section carved upon them.

FIG 9.4: *Although there were few gravestones before the mid-17th century most churchyards would have had a cross marking the consecrated ground. These prominent symbols were usually erected upon a stepped base but were easy targets for destruction in the century after the Restoration and few remain intact. What is commonly found, however, is the worn base on the south side of the church, sometimes with a Georgian sundial or Victorian replacement for the original cross mounted on top.*

FIG 9.5 CORBRIDGE, NORTHUMBERLAND: *A humble residence for the incumbent was a common feature in the medieval period before more spacious vicarages and rectories were built. Most were probably of timber and are long since gone but this notable stone example at Corbridge survives. It was a fortified tower house to protect those inside from Scottish raiders, built around 1300 and had room on the ground floor so the priest could drive in his cattle and then use the floors above for accommodation.*

FIG 9.6: *Lych gates are the point where the coffin bearers traditionally had to wait for the priest to welcome the deceased onto the consecrated land. Most today have a timber gable roof, gates and occasionally a bench or slab for the coffin to be placed upon, and they date from the last two centuries though some are older if only in part. This was an important feature as many remote chapels did not have consecrated burial grounds until the 19th century and the funeral procession had a five or ten mile walk along so-called 'corpse roads' to get to a churchyard.*

Gravestones began to be erected especially after the Restoration of the Monarchy in 1660, of simple design at first, then by the Georgian period more elaborate until in Victorian times a wide range of monuments of more affordable price began bursting the limits of the churchyard.

The boom in the population and the still hideous death rate in some areas around the turn of the 19th century put excessive strain on urban churchyards. Graves had always been dug through older burials but now the demand was such that God's Acre was inadequate and new sites were required. This encouraged speculators to offer private burial grounds as an alternative though many of these were no more than a chapel with hundreds and even thousands of coffins literally stacked up and rotting away in the basement. The stench was intolerable and the service provided so poor that the numerous complaints coupled with concerns about public health resulted in the banning of burials within a church from the late 1840s. The important members of the community now found themselves out in the open and so they created ever more elaborate Gothic memorials to differentiate themselves from the common gravestones around. New landscaped private cemeteries were an alternative for the better off and after legislation in the 1850s public versions set in similar parkland were laid out on the edge of most towns and cities. The problem with overcrowding was in part alleviated with the legalization of cremation after 1885.

Graves and Memorials

Like the church itself, Christian graves are aligned from east to west, a distinguishing factor when archaeologists excavate Saxon burial grounds (earlier pagan Saxon graves do not have a set orientation). One reason for this is believed to be that at the Second Coming the dead will awake and face the rising sun in the east; however, this alignment is not unique to Christian graves and there may be

FIG 9.7 LONG MELFORD, SUFFOLK: *It is common to see a rectangular field added on to the side of the original churchyard to increase burial space in the past century or two, mainly in rural locations. When the old boundary is removed between the two a bank usually remains so you have to step down into the new undisturbed plot. This has often been enhanced by the displacement of soil caused by constant reburials over maybe a thousand years, which has raised the level of the churchyard sometimes by as much as five or six feet over the surrounding land. Trenches around the church have often been created by the same action.*

other long forgotten reasons associated with sun worship.

The cold and shaded north side of the churchyard was unpopular and associated with evil so medieval burials were rare (it is likely that this area was used for entertainment and fairs due to this lack of graves). Later it was often used for strangers, suicides and unbaptized children, until the 18th and 19th centuries when pressure for space put it into general use. The sunnier south, especially around the east end ('as near to the altar as you could' was just as relevant outside as within the church) was seen as the best spot and is usually where the better off were buried.

It is still the practice to reuse plots, sometimes after as little as 100 years. Although you would expect to find the oldest graves close to the building and the more modern further away, this regular digging through old graves means that Victorian memorials can often be found next to the church and then any older Georgian gravestones which were never reused a little further out.

Pre-Victorian graves could vary greatly in depth with some barely more than a foot deep. Paupers often had their coffins collected in a large shallow pit which was only covered up when sufficiently full. It was also the practice for the text on the gravestone to face away from the burial, often with a smaller foot-stone to mark the other end, until the mid-19th century when it was reversed to look over it. Foot-stones are rarely found in situ now but have been re-positioned to rest up against the headstone. To make mowing the grass easier it is common for old gravestones to be re-sited up against the boundary wall.

Gravestones

Gravestones are the most characteristic feature of the modern churchyard, packed with information about families, life expectancy and society at the time of burial. The text on some slates can seem remarkably fresh even after centuries (the best survivors are in the Midlands and South-West); other stones, however, weather and split, with the shape and size of the stone the best clues to date it (the spread of lichens can also be used to date stones as they grow so slowly).

FIG 9.8 YOULGREAVE, DERBYS:
Some of the earliest gravestones from the late 17th century were no more than a short thick stone with the initials and date of death. Larger ones had text as above but clumsily laid out with words split between lines.

The availability of materials and the cost of a mason made gravestones rare before the late 17th century and only common in the 19th when transport costs dropped and workshops became widespread. Even then it was still a large outlay for poorer families which could often only be achieved through clubs and societies.

The earliest gravestones which you are likely to find in churchyards today will date from just after the Restoration in 1660, and these are rare, with many having nothing earlier than the 18th

FIG 9.10: *Details from Georgian gravestones from Long Sutton, Lincs. Skulls and angels or cherubs' heads remained popular in the first half of the 18th century before the full bodied variety of the latter became more common. Honour and glory could be symbolized by the crown, often with clouds, while the dove was a popular centrepiece in the last quarter of the century. The trumpet was also a widely used symbol heralding victory and resurrection.*

FIG 9.9: *The head of an early 18th-century gravestone with symbols reflecting the morbid obsession with time and mortality. A common symbol used in the late 17th and early 18th centuries is the skull and crossbones, not a pirate's burial but a sign for mortality used at least since the medieval period on memorials (the skull and two thigh bones are believed to be the parts of the body required for the resurrection). Hourglasses remind us of our mortality and angels or a cherub's head with wings represent the soul flying up to heaven, and sometimes a symbol of the deceased's trade, like a sheaf of corn for a farmer, was used.*

century. Most of these early stones were only a few feet high, some no more than posts or stubby, thick slabs, often with just the initials of the deceased. On more elaborate examples the head of the stone contains crude symbols associated with mortality and time under a hood mould or scrolls while the text below is often clumsily fitted in. Most will have sunken so appear shorter than when originally set and this can often obscure the dates and other information at the bottom.

Georgian gravestones develop from these early decorative types into a flourish of Rococo style during the mid century and later more refined Greek Revival in the Regency period. The size of the slab grew in some cases up to 6 ft tall and the profile of the head changed from elaborate curves to more simple geometric shapes by the early 19th century. Locally established masons were now more widespread and designed a wide range of beautifully decorated memorials for the better off members of society, some even coloured with paint and gilt, although this faded often in just a matter of months.

There was also a change in social attitudes towards the grave in the early 19th century; no longer was it just a place where the body was deposited but was now seen as the property of the family, which they would regularly visit, and could be defined by railings or stone kerbs. The symbols at the top became less gruesome, with elegant ladies weeping under willows and an urn often with fabric draped around it the most common from the late 18th century through to the mid 19th.

FIG 9.11: *Rococo style gravestone with deep foliage and convex centrepiece.*

FIG 9.12: *The Greek Revival style of architecture began influencing gravestone design from the 1770s and the distinctive shallow Classical decoration with symbols like the urn, medallions and Greek key were popular through the Regency period. As in this picture, a mourning figure (still referred to as a weeper) under a willow with an urn was a common arrangement.*

The reinvigorated Church of England and the Gothic Revival of the 1840s began to influence the design of memorials. They reviled the ornate Georgian classical gravestones and promoted plain slabs made from local materials and featuring the cross (something which had been absent since the Reformation for fear of Popery), accompanied by a healthy donation to the church. They had some effect in urban churchyards but less so in the country. In the new municipal cemeteries the Gothic style was incorporated alongside the Classical, but discretion was not the order of the day, and elaborate gravestones, rustic crosses, and weeping angels standing above a grave framed by a cast iron surround or stone kerb dominated. Imported white marble memorials from Italy were increasingly popular and cheaper than domestic versions, taking work from local quarries, while

FIG 9.14: *There was a wide range of Victorian gravestones although most had a steep pointed Gothic arch as above. Crosses and weeping angels were also popular. The 19th-century text is usually heavier, more regular and deeply incised than the ornate and flowing Georgian types, and highlighted in lead, black or gilt. A wide range of different stones characterizes Victorian graveyards and it was common for them to be mixed in one memorial or feature insets of brass or tiles.*

FIG 9.13: *Double gravestones with two profiled tops were usually made for husbands and wives or other family members. However, in this case the other half was never completed, making you wonder what happened to poor Augustine's wife after his demise!*

architect-designed gravestones were produced en masse in towns, taking trade from local masons already struggling with a shrinking rural client base (reorganization of villages meant fewer wealthy landowners).

Ledgers, Mausoleums and Tombs

An important grave in the past could have been marked by something more elaborate than just a gravestone, ranging from a ledger (a horizontal slab) to elaborate chest tombs or occasionally even a family mausoleum. In the Saxon and early medieval period only ecclesiastics were usually permitted to be buried within the church so there would have probably been some wooden and stone carved memorials in the churchyard for laymen. During the medieval period a stone slab with a simple cross running its full length was a common memorial for important members of the community inside and outside the church. Coped stones, resembling a squat cruciform church, with text running down the sides or raised to form gabled house tombs were used into the 17th century, and then revived by the Gothic-obsessed Victorians.

Chest tombs have a ledger raised up upon a hollow rectangular stone box with the grave in the ground below. These most splendid of churchyard memorials can be found dating back to the early 17th century and occasionally before but are commonly from the 18th century.

Some are no more than a flat ledger raised upon the chest, featuring a few pillars, but the more decorative examples can have elaborate figures supporting panels in the sides. The style of these features very much follows those of gravestones except the figures are in full rather than just the head, with deeper, richly carved work from the late 17th to mid-18th centuries followed by shallow Greek Revival

FIG 9.15: *Flat slabs known as ledgers set horizontally over the grave can be found flush with the ground or raised upon a plinth and are common from the mid-17th century onwards. These are more likely to have most of their inscriptions exposed compared with gravestones which have usually partially sunk. This example comes from Cheshire, a county along with Lancashire where it was common for them to be laid in a row along paths. Note the different text, showing how a family has reused the plot over more than 100 years.*

patterns through to the early Victorian period. The Victorians, however, preferred the emphasis on the vertical and although there are chest tombs richly decorated with Gothic symbols, the obelisk, pillar and shrine memorials are more common, especially in cemeteries.

FIG 9.16: *Late 17th- and early 18th-century chest tombs. The oldest types tend to have a large, heavy slab on top and a thin body (top) with finer examples having decorated sides. These usually have pilasters to the sides and figures surrounding a central plaque (bottom) with the details reflecting the obsession with symbols of mortality and architectural fashion.*

FIG 9.17: *The finest chest tombs from the 17th and 18th centuries are to be found in the Cotswolds. Those in the eastern part tend to have a peculiar semi-circular slab across the top, known as a Bale Tomb (top) from the wool-bale used by the merchants who tend to be the main occupants of the graves. However, it is more likely to represent the medieval hearse, a curved cage built over the body to support the pall (funeral cloth). In the western part the Flamboyant Tomb (bottom) is common, which has a thick plain slab but richly-carved side panels, often with a couple of scrolls at the ends.*

FIG 9.18: *Late 18th- and early 19th-century tombs are decorated with delicate Neo-Classical patterns and details. A table tomb, a horizontal ledger supported on stone columns, was often used in the northern counties.*

FIG 9.19: *Occasionally a wealthy local family would choose to bury themselves and their heirs in a mausoleum set in the churchyard. Most of those found date from the 18th century as in this example from Stone, Staffordshire.*

FIG 9.20: *Victorian tombs had a clear emphasis on the vertical and were highly decorated with Gothic pointed arches, columns and capitals. They could range from the simple obelisk to ostentatious multi-tiered piles capped with a spire. Some were even made from cast iron (right) and most would have been surrounded by railings (often ripped up for scrap metal in the Second World War).*

Section III

Quick
Reference
Guide

With such a wonderful variety of English churches it can be somewhat bewildering when first approaching one, when there will be so much that is unique to the building. This book can give you a basic grounding but if you wish to better understand a particular church then applying this knowledge is best done in a systematic fashion. Work from the whole to the part, look at the surroundings, the churchyard and the main structure before studying its detail.

Location

If the church is in the centre of the village or oldest part of a town, then it could be an early foundation. If it is remote but next to a large house or farm, then it too could be ancient, it's just that the village has moved away. The building next to it is worth noting; a highly decorative church is often found to have had a bishop or abbot as a neighbour.

Churchyard

A roughly circular plan to a churchyard

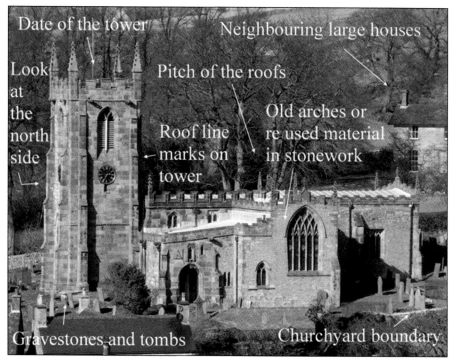

Date of the tower

Neighbouring large houses

Look at the north side

Pitch of the roofs

Roof line marks on tower

Old arches or re-used material in stonework

Gravestones and tombs

Churchyard boundary

FIG 10.1: *Some of the features, in addition to the style of the details, to look for when studying a church.*

is an indication of an ancient foundation, although not a conclusive one, as is the presence of old barrows and standing stones. The build-up of soil from digging graves over the centuries can create a step up from surrounding areas and a retaining wall around the building, a sign again of an old church. Note the age of memorials; the church might be Victorian but older gravestones can tell you that there was another church before it on the site.

Structure

Note the arrangement of the parts and their general proportions. Tall, narrow naves and chancels are a sign of Saxon or Norman work although they are usually hidden behind later aisles and chapels. Central towers were popular up to the 13th century, west ones became dominant in the 14th and 15th. Original roofs were steep pitched and thatched, but were often replaced by lower pitched ones, leaving a mark on the east side of the tower (and sometimes the chancel remains at the original pitch as well).

Walk all around the church; never ignore the shaded north side as this is often where the best clues are to the age of the church. Note blocked doors and windows, the shape of the arch indicating its date. Faint arches in the stonework can indicate old aisles which have been blocked as the congregation reduced. Look at the stonework; if it is patchy and of differing quality then it will probably be old, if the whole building looks to be of the same with a neat plinth all around then it is most likely Georgian or Victorian. If the stonework is fine-cut ashlar then it is a sign of great wealth. If it is brick then it will usually be 15th-century at the earliest; thin, irregular bricks laid with no clear pattern date from this period, but have a definite bonding by the 17th century and are of regular size by the 18th.

Details inside can be just as important as those outside. The chancel arch and aisle arcades will often be older than the exterior would lead you to believe. The shapes of windows, style of decoration and the fittings within can help, but remember that most of these parts could be moved from other sites, like a monastery after the Dissolution or a neighbouring church when it closed due to falling numbers.

Name

The dedication in memory of a popular saint or event can be of note. Saxon names can indicate an early foundation while St Paul and Holy Trinity were popular Victorian names. The most common medieval church names were St Mary, All Saints, St Peter, St Michael, St Andrew and St John the Baptist.

Taking it further

Should you wish to find out more about a specific building then more detailed information should be available. Here are some suggestions:

* Booklet for sale inside the church.

* The *Buildings of England* series, initially by Nikolaus Pevsner. Each county is separately covered with details on the churches of every town and

village at the beginning of each entry.

* The *Victoria County History* is a series of county-based books in which historians do all the hard work of translating and listing historic documents relating to a manor. Not every county is covered yet but if it has been completed then the library will hold a copy.

* Internet: Most churches have a site, although using a search engine can usually reveal more. Family History sites can be useful, especially about memorials.

* Listings: Most buildings will be listed and libraries often hold the study by local architectural historians

when the listing was made.

* Records of the original builder like an abbey, bishop or lord of the manor will have information if available, and those responsible for the church today may also have details.

* Local history groups may hold information. In many abandoned churches archaeological digs may have taken place revealing a detailed history of its development. The reports should be available through the local library.

* Memorials or old graveslabs could indicate an early date. Look for some broken pieces built into later walls.

FIG 10.2 WHARRAM PERCY, YORKS: *This deserted medieval village still has the remains of its medieval parish church (top left) which, as the area has been intensively studied over the past 50 years, has a detailed building history making it worth a visit to see how churches developed and declined. Details include the filled-in arcade (top right), reused graveslabs (bottom left), and rubble core of walls (bottom right).*

A timechart showing some of the key features and decorative details which can be used to date medieval churches.

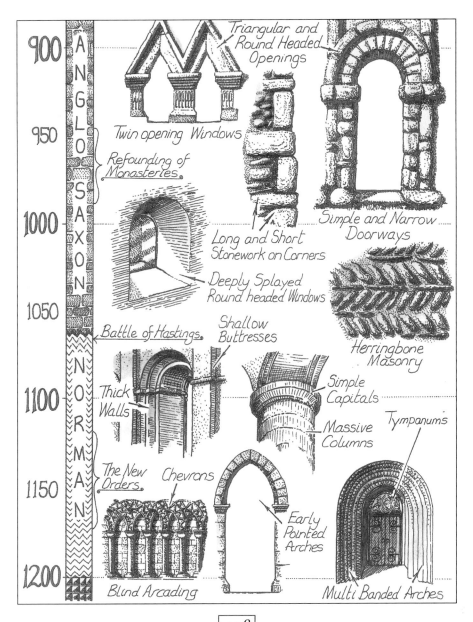

900

ANGLO

Triangular and Round Headed Openings

950

Twin opening Windows

Refounding of Monasteries.

1000

Long and Short Stonework on Corners

Simple and Narrow Doorways

Deeply Splayed Round headed Windows

1050

SAXON

Battle of Hastings.

Shallow Buttresses

Herringbone Masonry

1100

NORMAN

Thick Walls

Simple Capitals

Massive Columns

Tympanums

1150

The New Orders.

Chevrons

Early Pointed Arches

1200

Blind Arcading

Multi Banded Arches

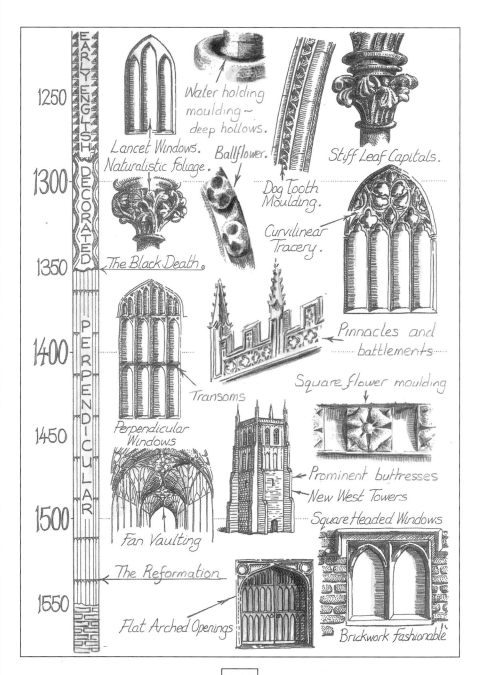

EARLY ENGLISH

DECORATED

PERPENDICULAR

1250

1300

1350

1400

1450

1500

1550

Lancet Windows. Naturalistic foliage.

Water holding moulding ~ deep hollows.

Ballflower.

Dog Tooth Moulding.

Stiff Leaf Capitals.

Curvilinear Tracery.

The Black Death.

Pinnacles and battlements.

Transoms

Square flower moulding

Perpendicular Windows

Prominent buttresses

New West Towers

Square Headed Windows

Fan Vaulting

The Reformation

Flat Arched Openings

Brickwork Fashionable

Below are listed just a few churches of note which have featured in this book (with the fig no. of where they are pictured), including postcode (for your Sat Nav) and/or grid reference (go to www.ordnancesurvey.com and put the grid reference into the 'Get a Map' service to find location).

Aldgate, London (Fig 4.17), St Botolph without Aldgate, Aldgate High St, EC3N 1AB: TQ 335812
Ashbourne, Derbys (Fig 7.16, 7.21), St Oswald, Mayfield Rd: SK 176464
Ashwell, Herts (Fig 3.22), St Mary the Virgin: TL 267397
Astbury, Cheshire (Fig 3.18, 8.12), St Mary: SJ 846615
Backwell, Somerset (Fig 8.14), St Andrew, Church Lane, BS48 3JJ: ST 492/683
Bakewell, Derbys (Fig 1.25, 7.14, 7.15, 9.3), All Saints, South Church St, DE45 1FD: SK 215684
Barnack, Cambs (Fig 8.8), St John the Baptist: TF 079050
Barton-upon-Humber, Lincs (Fig 8.4), St Peter: TA 035219
Birmingham, West Midlands (Fig 4.8), St Philip's Cathedral, Colmore Row, B3 2QB: SP 069870
Boston, Lincs (Fig 2.14, 7.13, 8.2), St Botolph: TF 326441
Brixworth, Northants (Fig 0.1, 1.3, 1.19), All Saints, Church St: SP 757712
Brockhampton-by-Ross, Hereford (Fig 5.14, 5.19), All Saints: SO 594321
Burford, Oxon (Fig 1.11, 3.5), St John the Baptist, Church Green, OX18 4RY: SP 253124
Bylaugh, Norfolk (Fig 8.3), St Mary, NR20 4QE: TG 036183
Cawston, Norfolk (Fig 3.19), St Agnes, Church Lane, NR10 4AG: TG 133239
Cheadle, Staffs (Fig 5.8), St Giles (RC): SK 008432
Chipping Campden, Glos (Fig 3.16), St James, Church St, GL55 6JG: SP 154395
Dunstable, Beds (Fig 4.2), St Peter (Priory Church of): TL 021218
Earls Barton, Northants (Fig 1.20), All Saints, West Street: SP 852638
Easby, North Yorks (Fig 6.13), St Agatha (Easby Abbey): NZ 185003
Empingham, Leics (Fig 2.2), St Peter, Church St, LE15 8PN: SK 950085
Escomb, County Durham (Fig 1.18), St John: NZ 189301
Felmersham, Beds (Fig 2.21, 7.6), St Mary, Church End, MK43 7JP: SP 991578
Fingest, Bucks (Fig 8.6), St Bartholomew, RG9 6QE: SU 777911
Gibside, County Durham (Fig 4.9), Gibside Chapel, St Wulfram, NE16 6BG: NZ 172583
Grantham, Lincs (Fig 8.13), : SK 915361
Greensted-juxta-Ongar, Essex (Fig 1.17, 8.11), St Andrew, CM5 9LD: TL 538030
Hampstead Garden Suburb, London (Fig 5.17), St Jude-on-the-Hill, Central Square, NW11 7AH: TQ 255883
Heckington, Lincs (Fig 2.25, 7.12), St Andrew: TF 143441
Hexham, Northumberland (Fig 2.27), St Andrew (Hexham Abbey), Beaumont St, NE46 3NB: NY 934640

Kegworth, Leics (Fig 2.22), St Andrew, Churchgate, DE74 2ED: SK 487267

Kempley, Glos (Fig 6.12), St Mary: SO 670312

Ketton, Rutland (Fig 2.4), St Mary the Virgin : SK 982043

Kilpeck, Hereford (Fig 1.9, 1.13, 1.22), St Mary and St David: SO445305

Kirby Bellars, Leics (Fig 8.9), St Peter, Main St, LE14 2EE: SK 718182

Lavenham, Suffolk (Fig 3.3, 3.6, 3.21), St Peter and St Paul, Church St, CO10 9QT: TL 913490

Long Melford, Suffolk (Fig 3.14, 9.7), Holy Trinity, Church Walk, CO10 9DL: TL 865467

Long Sutton, Lincs (Fig 9.10), St Mary, Market Place, PE12 9JJ: TF 432229

Monkwearmouth, Sunderland (Fig 8.5), St Peter, St Peters Way, SR6 0DY: NZ 401578

Nantwich, Cheshire (Fig 2.23, 6.20), St Mary, Church Lane: SJ 652523

Newcastle upon Tyne (Fig 4.18), All Saints: NZ 253640

North Runcton, Norfolk (Fig 4.15), All Saints, The Green, PE33 0RB: TF 646159

Repton, Derbys (Fig 7.2), St Wystan: DE65 6FH: SK 302271

Rudston, Yorks (Fig 9.2), All Saints: TA 098677

Shrewsbury, Shropshire (Fig 4.14), St Chad, Claremont Bank: SJ 488124

Stamford, Lincs (Fig 2.20), St Mary, St Marys Hill, PE9 2DF: TF 030070

Steetley, Derbys (Fig 1.10), All Saints Chapel: SK543787

Stewkley, Bucks (Fig 1.21) St Michael and All Angels, High St North, LU7 0HL: SP 852261

Stow, Lincs (Fig 1.2, 1.23), St Mary: SK 882820

Studley Royal, Ripon (Fig 5.15, 5.20), St Mary, West Yorks, HG4 3DY: SE 275693

Thurton, Norfolk (Fig 2.24), St Ethelbert: TG 328007

Tickencote, Rutland (Fig 1.24), St Peter: SK 990095

Tong, Shropshire (Fig 3.20, 7.8), St Bartholomew, TF11 8PW: SJ 796074

Warwick (Fig 7.3), St Mary, Old Square, CV34 4AB: SP 282649

Westerham, Kent (Fig 2.1), St Mary the Virgin, The Green, TN16 1AS: TQ 447541

West Walton, Norfolk (Fig 2.5, 2.19), St Mary: TF 471134

West Wycombe, Bucks (Fig 4.4), St Lawrence, West Wycombe Hill, HP14 3AP: SU 827949

Wharram Percy, Yorks (Fig 10.2): SE 859644

Whitby, North Yorks (Fig 6.16), St Mary, Church St, YO22 4JT: NZ 901113

Winscombe, Somerset (Fig 3.2, 8.14), St James the Great, Church Lane, BS25 1DE: ST 411566

Witley Court, Worcs (Fig 4.7, 4.19), Great Witley church, WR6 6JT: SO 769649

Wrington, Somerset (Fig 3.17), All Saints, Station Road, BS40 5LG: ST 467627

Youlgreave, Derbys (Fig 8.15, 9.8), All Saints: SK 212643

AISLE:	The side wings behind the rows of columns (arcade) supporting the main walls of the church.
ALTAR:	A flat topped table or block on which a sacrifice is made. It was the focal point of a medieval church as the sacrificial element of the mass was regarded as the most important. It could also hold relics.
AMBULATORY:	A passage running around the outside of a Saxon crypt (also used for the same role around the edge of a chancel in a large church or cathedral).
ANGLICAN:	Of the Church of England.
APSE:	A semi-circular or polygonal projection from the end of the chancel.
ARCADE:	A row of columns.
ASHLAR:	Smooth, squared masonry with fine joints.
AUMBRY:	A cupboard recessed into the wall (usually missing its wooden door today).
BALUSTER:	A turned post supporting a horizontal rail (in a row they form a balustrade).
BEAKHEADS:	Ornamental carvings of the heads of birds and beasts with painted beaks, which can be found around arches on Norman churches.
BELFRY:	The part of the tower in which the bells are held. Usually identified on the outside by louvred belfry openings.
BONDING:	The way bricks are laid in a wall with the different patterns on the outer surface formed by headers (short ends) and stretchers (long sides).
BUTTRESS:	A projecting stack of masonry set at right angles to a wall in order to support it.
CAPITAL:	The head or top of a column, often decorated.
CHANCEL:	The part of the church containing the altar (usually the eastern end). In larger churches the chancel is subdivided into a choir and presbytery, sometimes with a passage running around the outside of these.
CHANTRY:	An altar or chapel where mass was chanted for its donor.
CHARNEL HOUSE OR PIT:	A site where bones were deposited from graves when they were cleared to make room for a new burial.
CLERESTORY:	The upper section of the wall in a nave which is usually fitted with windows.
COMMUNION TABLE:	In Anglican churches the emphasis of the service was upon the community meal and thus the altar was renamed or replaced by a communion table.

CORBEL:	A stone bracket set into a wall, often used to support roof trusses.
CROSSING:	The section of a church directly below a central tower.
CRYPT:	A chamber below the floor of a church for holding a grave or relic.
DORMER:	An upright window set into the angle of a roof.
ENCAUSTIC:	Tiles with different colours inlaid into patterns which are burnt in.
FAÇADE:	The main vertical face of a building.
FONT:	A basin containing holy water used for baptism.
GABLE:	The pointed upper section of a wall at the end of a pitched roof.
GROIN:	The edge where two vaults meet.
HAMMER-BEAM:	A type of roof truss using a system of hammer posts, beams and brackets without any horizontal timber running across the full width of the church.
HERRINGBONE:	Stone or brickwork laid in alternating diagonal layers (a zig-zag, in effect).
IMPOST:	A moulded piece of brick or masonry from which an arch springs.
JAMBS:	The sides of an opening for a door or window.
KEYSTONE:	The top, central stone in a arch.
LADY CHAPEL:	A chapel dedicated to the Virgin Mary.
LANCET:	A tall narrow window with a pointed arch which was popular in the 13th century (often set in threes or fives).
LECTERN:	A small angled desk upon an upright post used to hold books (usually gilt metal in the shape of an eagle with outstretched wings).
LIERNE:	A short rib connecting the joints of the principal ribs on a stone-vaulted ceiling.
LINTEL:	A horizontal supporting beam set above a door or window.
LOUVRE:	Slanted slats, in the case of a church used across the belfry openings.
MASS:	The common name for the Eucharist, the central act of Christian worship.
MINSTER:	The name for a monastic church which despatched priests over a set area in the Anglo-Saxon period before parishes were formed. The name was retained by some up to the present day even though their role has changed.
MISERICORD:	A decorated projection on the underside of flip-down seats on which the person standing in front could rest during long services (from Latin *misericordia* meaning mercy).
MOULDING:	A decorative strip of stone, brick or plaster.

MULLION:	A vertical bar in a window.
NAVE:	The main body of the church where the congregation stand or sit (usually the larger western portion).
OGEE:	A curved line with a concave lower section and convex upper (a reversed 'S' shape) which form a distinctive arch popular in the 14th and 15th centuries.
PARAPET:	The top section of wall above the sloping end of a roof.
PEDIMENT:	A low pitched triangular feature above the entrance on a Classical building.
PILASTER:	A flat column fixed to a wall.
PINNACLE:	A small pointed turret used as decoration or to add weight on top of a tower, wall or buttress.
PISCINA:	A stone basin for washing communion vessels.
PITCH:	The angle at which a roof slopes. A plain sloping roof of two sides is called a pitched roof.
PLINTH:	A projecting base around a building.
PORTICO:	A structure forming a porch over a doorway, usually with a flat roof supported on columns and used on Classical churches especially in the late 18th and early 19th centuries.
PRESBYTERY:	The part of the church where the high altar stood (usually only referred to as such in larger churches with a choir).
PULPIT:	A raised structure from which a sermon is preached.
REFORMATION, THE:	The reforming of the church in the early 16th century but which is used here for the foundation of the Church of England and the break with the Papacy by Henry VIII in 1531.
RENDER:	A protective covering for a wall.
REREDOS:	A stone screen on the east wall behind the altar.
RESTORATION, THE:	The return of the monarchy to the throne in 1660.
ROOD:	The cross or crucifix which was originally mounted on top of the screen between the nave and chancel.
SACRISTY:	A room used for storing sacred vessels (usually associated with medieval churches (a vestry is used for this in the Church of England).
SCREEN:	A decorated wooden or stone partition between two parts of a building (usually dividing the nave from the chancel in a church).
SEDILIA:	Seats for the senior members of the clergy, usually a set of three recessed into the south wall next to the altar.
SQUINT:	A small opening in a wall to give someone in another part of the church a clear view of the altar.
STALLS:	Rows of seats or benches, sometimes with elaborate carved canopies at the western end of the chancel (the choir) and

used by senior members of the clergy (used by choirs only since the 19th century).

STOUP: A basin with holy water, near the entrance of the church.

STRING COURSE: A horizontal band running across a façade and usually projecting from it.

TRACERY: The ornamental masonry pieces making patterns in the upper part of arched windows or belfry openings.

TRANSEPTS: The short arms of a church projecting north and south from the crossing.

TRANSOM: A horizontal bar in a window (usually a feature of large Perpendicular windows).

TRIFORIUM: A row of arches above the arcade and below the clerestory in large Norman churches.

TRUSS: A series of beams forming a triangular frame to support the roof timbers. The ends either rest upon the walls or on stone brackets (corbels).

TYMPANUM: The space within an arch above a doorway which was usually decorated in Norman churches.

VAULT: An arched ceiling of stone or brick (when supported by thin lengths of masonry it is known as rib vaulting).

VERNACULAR: Buildings made from local materials in styles and construction methods passed down within a distinct geographical area.

VESTRY: A room where vestments are stored (also used for storing vessels etc in the Church of England; many are Victorian or modern additions).

VOUSSOIR: A wedge-shaped segment which makes up an arch.

BIBLIOGRAPHY

Pevsner, Nikolaus (and others), *The Buildings of England* series: covers each county with detailed architectural reviews of all churches.

Blatch, Mervyn, *Parish Churches of England* (1974)
Jones, Lawrence E., *The Observer's Book of Old English Churches* (1965)
Murray, Peter & Linda, *The Oxford Companion to Christian Art and Architecture* (1998)
Platt, Colin, *The Parish Churches of Medieval England* (1995)
Rodwell, Warwick, *The Archaeology of the English Church* (1981)

INDEX

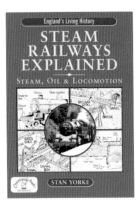

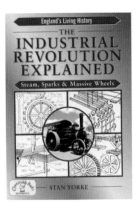

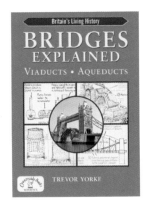

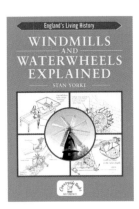

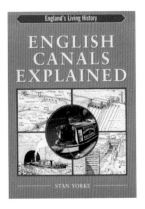

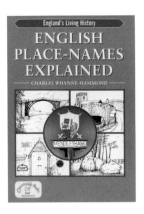

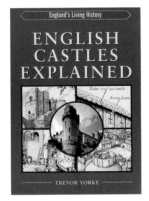

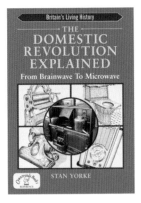